C000262722

THE INGLEWOOD WAY·TO·HEALTH

THE INGLEWOOD WAY·TO·HEALTH

ANTOINETTE MOSES

DAVID & CHARLES
NEWTON ABBOT · LONDON

Food photography by Robert Green and Stephen Wilson

British Library Cataloguing in Publication Data
Moses, Antoinette
The Inglewood way to health.
1. Physical fitness. Slimming diet. 2. Slimmers. Food – Recipes
I. Title II. Inglewood, Firm
613.2′5

ISBN 0-7153-9388-X

Phototypeset by Typesetters (Birmingham) Ltd, Smethwick, West Midlands
and printed in Portugal by Resopal
for David & Charles Publishers plc
Brunel House Newton Abbot Devon

·Contents·

·Foreword·

EATING YOUR WAY TO HEALTH

Inglewood Health Hydro enjoys a national, even international, reputation as Britain's premier residential centre for weight reduction, stress relief and the promotion of physical fitness. Its regime of diet and exercise under medical supervision has proved to be especially successful, both remedially and as a contribution to preventative medicine. This is acknowledged by the privileged men and women who regularly stay at the splendid mansion in its secluded forty acres of parkland on the fringe of the Berkshire Downs.

However, not everyone is able to stay and enjoy the Inglewood experience which involves a range of such specialist treatments as massage, physiotherapy, Slendertone, osteopathy, aroma-therapy and reflexology. As befits a hydro, there is a variety of baths – Turkish, sauna, whirlpool, impulse, moor, wax and more. The gymnasium, heated swimming pool and other amenities also figure in the day's routine.

However, a key factor is natural diet, and this can be followed at home. It is to introduce the delights and benefits of this diet to a wider public that this book has been compiled by one of the beneficiaries with the help of the kitchen and clinical staff.

At Inglewood, the regime means mainly fresh, pure vegetables and salads, many grown in the estate's own gardens and served at the hydro's famous salad buffets. But the ingredients are available everywhere, and the tested recipes published here ensure that you will always find them as tasty as they are wholesome.

Inglewood's goal is to add years of activity to guests' lives while removing years from their faces and figures. This book aims to do the same. It will certainly add new pleasure to your meals, fresh excitement to your palate and good nutrition to your life style. Bon appetit!

Surely one of the most pleasant ways of exercising – enjoying Inglewood's superb heated pool

·The·Inglewood·Way·

Dr Peter Hetherington MA(Cantab) MB B Chir MRCGP DRCOG

If you are reading this book – perhaps you are perusing a copy in a bookshop – you are probably unhappy about your size or state of fitness. Go on reading, because this is a book that can change your life and help you become slimmer and fitter. How does our plan succeed, you wonder, where so many diets have failed? It is because we believe that you should enjoy life. With a host of delicious low-calorie recipes and an eating plan for life instead of short-term diets, plus exercises to make you feel good, we make getting into shape a *positive* pleasure.

We are positive also about the need to get in shape. If you are overweight you may already find yourself short of breath and suffering from backache or find that your feet swell in summer but you are also making yourself liable to illnesses like chest trouble, gallstones, high blood pressure, diabetes, heart attack and strokes. You are also more likely to have complications after an operation and for women difficulties in pregnancy. All these are on top of the social problems of being overweight, finding it hard to find clothes which fit, feeling embarrassed about your size on a beach or even hiding your body from your partner.

These are problems which so often face the really overweight, those suffering from obesity. And if you think you might be fat but obesity is something that happens to other people, have a look at Table A (p19) compiled by the Royal College of Physicians.

So, you may not be obese but just overweight. But did you know that even mild degrees of overweight are now considered bad for our health? Doctors studying this problem, who previously thought that only the severely obese ran health risks, have now found that there is a progressive increase in illness and fatal illness apparent with only small increases above an acceptable weight. So we need to get into shape for the sake of our health, quite apart from the social pressures which may make us want to be slimmer and fitter.

OVERWEIGHT: THE REASONS

There are a great many reasons why people become overweight and we still don't understand all of them. To start with there are our genes. The shape we inherit from our parents and grandparents together with all our other inherited factors (which can also include a tendency towards heart disease and high blood pressure) derive from the genes we are born with. Then there are environmental factors which start from the day we are born. Eating patterns begin young and while we are born with an instinct which tells us when we are hungry, ie when we need to eat in order to stay alive, this is all too soon replaced by appetite. Appetite is an emotional trigger and quite a complicated one. From a young age we can associate food with comfort and love and therefore demand more than we actually need. And we go on setting up the same patterns with our own children. Perhaps, when we were small children and we fell over and hurt ourselves, we were given a sweet to 'take the pain away' and stop us crying. A dangerous habit to start!

Gradually as we get older we eat because of the time of day; it's lunchtime so we eat whether or not we are hungry. We eat when our tastebuds are stimulated by smell or sight; we buy a loaf of freshly baked bread and eat far too much of it because it smells so good. Sometimes we even stimulate our appetites by drinking aperitifs. In addition, we eat because of emotional triggers, often the ones that were set off in childhood. Emotional triggers are often at the root of the eating disorders that cause overweight in many of my patients. In order to get a sense of order back into their eating patterns I have to make them investigate why they became overweight and why, in so many cases, they use food as an emotional crutch.

But not everyone who is overweight has a psychological reason for this. If you eat just one slice of bread and butter more than you burn up each day over a period of ten years you could put on an extra 50kg (that's around 8 stone!) and it would take more than a slice of bread and butter less to lose that surplus weight. But it can be lost. The joy about the Inglewood plan is that it works – for everyone who follows it. This is because it is flexible enough to be adapted to any lifestyle and because it is based on solid, sensible, good nutrition and exercise and is not an 'instant' diet, one that puts the weight back on again as 'instantly' as you lost it.

A recent medical study showed that currently 65 per cent of British women and 30 per cent of British men were trying to lose weight. Many of these people have been trying to lose weight for years; perhaps you are one of them. You try one diet after another and start well, gradually get bored with it, fall by the wayside and go back to square one. Well, that is in the past. The Inglewood Plan is not a diet. It is a way of thinking fit. It is a way of eating to satisfy hunger and for enjoyment of food and not because of other triggers. It is a way of learning to enjoy exercise and revel in the pleasure of a better shape, a livelier attitude and having more energy.

We have included menu plans that contain only a limited number of calories but even these can be varied and once you have reached your ideal weight and shape you do not give up the plan but simply increase staple foods such as bread and potatoes, fruit and vegetables to give you the right calorific basis for weight maintenance. The Inglewood Plan is not a diet but a lifetime's invitation to a healthier way of living. And a way of making that a longer lifetime.

THE INGLEWOOD PLAN – HOW IT WORKS

Like all sensible eating patterns the Inglewood Plan is based on the number of calories you eat in relation to the number of calories you burn up. So, firstly you probably want to know: What is a calorie?

What is a Calorie?

A calorie is a measure of energy. You cannot see a calorie or actually eat one (though you can see the results of eating too many). It is an abstract unit. To be precise it is the amount of energy which; if converted into heat, would raise the temperature of 1g of water through 1°C. To be technically correct, we should be using the term kilocalorie (1 kcal=1000 calories) which you may see on packets and cans, but by common usage the shorter term 'calorie' is adopted for simplicity.

If this sounds too scientific think of yourself as a steam train that needs steam to function. You have to feed fuel to produce the energy which makes the steam and sets the wheels going round. We need fuel which our bodies convert to energy and a calorie is simply the amount of energy that a particular bit of fuel will create when burned. So, we burn off the fuel by moving about (and don't burn off enough when we sit all day) and we eat things (rather more appetising than coal) to create that energy. That's all it is. It is a simple equation: if we take in more calories than we burn up, the remainder will be stored as fat. If we burn up more calories than we stoke up with, we will begin to burn up our fat reserves.

Of course not everything is simple. We do not know why some people burn up more calories than others – what we call their metabolic rate. The calorie intake that can make one maintain a steady weight can make another put on weight or even take it off. A great deal of research is going into this enigma at the moment but while scientists probe I can tell you that once you have found your own rate for maintaining weight, if you take in less calories and burn up more, you will lose weight. It is important that the two go side by side: eat less and exercise more.

How Many Calories?

As you may surmise from the previous paragraphs, there are no hard-and-fast rules. The standard (DHSS) rate for an average, moderately active woman aged 18–34 to maintain weight is 2,150 calories a day. For a man this becomes 2,900. However, I know many patients who will put on weight at these figures; again hereditary factors, height and metabolic rate all have a role to play. What I do find is that any

Enjoying a stimulating jacuzzi bath

woman will lose weight steadily on a daily intake of 1,000 calories (1,500 for a man). I never advise patients to go below this except for short periods under medical supervision. To lose weight steadily you should take in about 500 calories fewer than you burn up and you would have to be bedridden to burn up less than 1,000 calories a day. Exercise, of course, helps enormously. Not only do you burn up more calories while exercising but it is thought that the body continues to burn up calories at a faster rate after exercise. So a short work-out first thing every morning could set your metabolic engine turning away at a faster rate all day.

Exercise will also make you generally fitter; it acts as an anti-depressant and helps to lower body fat. And it can make you feel less like smoking, if you still persist in this unhealthy activity. Exercise is just as important as what you eat and I suggest you read Debbie Jenkins' introduction on page 32 as well as follow her routine.

If you follow her advice and also change to a healthier eating pattern you will begin steadily to lose weight. But don't be depressed if you lose weight slowly. It takes many months to lose a lot of weight and after an initial period of rapid weight loss (usually the first one or two weeks) the desirable rate of loss will only be 1 or 2lb (.5 or 1kg) a week. It depends on your build and how much weight you have to lose. If you have only a few pounds to lose this can be irritatingly difficult and slow and take four to five weeks. If you want to lose a stone (6kg) then you may make a rapid start, with a first week loss of as much as 4lb (2kg) followed by a steady loss over six to seven weeks and so on. If you have as much as 4 stone (25kg) to lose it could take a year of steady weight loss, despite a spectacular first week's loss of 9 to 10lb (4 to 4.5kg). Remember if you are losing you are winning!

Once you reach your ideal weight you will want to stay with the plan to keep slim and fit. You will find it feels so much better (quite apart from all the other bonuses) that you won't want to return to your old eating pattern. That is why we provide the ideas for so many delicious meals. We don't believe that you should feel deprived or bored. Because it is a permanent way of life we don't think that it's dreadful when you occasionally give in and eat a chocolate bar, a piece of cake or drink too much, as long as it is only occasionally. If you are trying to lose weight the odd lapse will just slow you up a bit and if you are maintaining your weight you probably now know how to adjust your plan to balance those extra calories. As long as you keep a careful eye on your weight and weigh yourself once a week (quite often enough) you will know how strict you need to be with yourself over the coming week. If you've put on a couple of pounds you will cut down a little to lose them. The important thing is not to put weight on two weeks running or you will find yourself back on an upward spiral. Just be careful. Once you have established a pattern you will find your body knows how much it needs and you will feed it accordingly.

WHAT KIND OF DIET?

In the West our diet has two basic defects; it contains too much fat and too much sugar. Over the years there have been many misleading theories about diet (they still continue to get publicity). One of the most dangerous was the slogan 'eat fat and grow slim'. This was a misreading of a low-carbohydrate diet that worked on the premise that if you ate less carbohydrate, ie bread and potatoes, you would eat less butter and fat. The diet did not allow for people who ate cheese like starving mice, swamped their salads with mayonnaise and served their spinach with a good amount of butter and a shake of parmesan. That is what the author of this book tells me she did on this diet. Not surprisingly her weight soared.

Today, more than at any previous time, however, doctors and nutritionists around the world are united in their approach to nutrition and health. Their consensus is that we eat too much fat and not enough fibre. This has been agreed in a major US Senate report which drew on evidence prepared by over 200 scientists from 23 countries who were studying the relationship between diet and heart disease and also by the Royal Society of Physicians' *Report on Obesity*, published in 1983. The scientist's recommendations for a healthy diet are:

1 Fewer total calories
2 Less fat
3 Less saturated fat
4 Less cholesterol
5 Relatively more poly-unsaturated fat
6 Less sugar
7 Less salt
8 More fibre
9 More starchy foods

Let us consider these points briefly. Firstly, fewer calories are necessary as has already been discussed.

Secondly, less fat. This is very important. You can cut down on fat in many ways: by grilling food instead of frying it, for example, and by using one of the oil-free salad dressings suggested in this book.

Thirdly, eat less saturated fat. Saturated fats are the solid, animal (including dairy) fats. These fats include butter, cream, high-fat cheese, especially cream cheese, and fat in meats. We, in the West, eat far too much saturated fat which is a crucial factor in creating too much cholesterol.

Fourth, although controversy still exists, a great many doctors believe that high levels of cholesterol are directly linked with heart disease, which currently kills more than 15,000 people in Britain each year and is the largest single cause of death in this country. Cholesterol is a waxy, fatty substance which can build up until it gradually clogs the arteries. By reducing the amount of saturated fats in your diet you will also lower the levels of cholesterol in your blood. To cut down on cholesterol you should try to limit yourself to three or less egg yolks a week although you can eat as many egg whites as you wish. The recipes and plans in this book are generally aimed at reducing cholesterol as well as fats and it makes sensible nutritional – and slimming – sense not to eat foods which are high in cholesterol.

Fifth, if you are trying to lose weight you will certainly not want to increase your consumption of fats, but when you do use fat you should switch to one that is high in polyunsaturates. Use a low-calorie spread instead of butter on your toast and sweat your onion in a little sunflower oil. But, generally, eat less fat.

Sixth, when you cut calories you automatically cut down on your sugar intake and even when maintaining your weight you should try to eat less sugar. You will eat plenty anyway as so many packaged foods already contain sugar, which is something your body has no real need for. It also destroys your teeth, so cut out sugary drinks, sugar added to fruit and in puddings, cakes, biscuits and sweets. If you have a sweet tooth you can use a low-calorie sweetener, but try to wean your tastebuds away from sweet food and cut down on all sugars.

Seventh, salt is not fattening but as a doctor I am aware of recent reports on the relationship between salt and blood pressure. The World Health Organisation (WHO) is one body that feels that the daily intake (currently thought to be 1oz/12g a day) should be lower. So don't put salt automatically in the water when cooking vegetables and try to cut down on the amount of table salt you use.

Finally, points 8 and 9 I shall discuss together. In the last year or two a lot of publicity has been given to the need to increase fibre in the diet and I am all for it! A high-fibre content in your diet can certainly help in eliminating such problems as constipation, piles, bowel diseases and diverticulitis. A healthy daily intake of fibre is now considered to be about ¾–1oz/(20–30g) and this should come from an increased consumption of wholegrain cereals. You will notice in all the Inglewood menu plans that you are given a reasonable daily allowance of wholemeal bread, wholewheat flour, wholewheat pasta and other staple carbohydrates. These do, in fact, with the fruit and vegetables suggested, add up to a daily allowance of ¾–1oz(20–30g) of fibre. It also means that the largest proportion of your diet is starchy food such as bread and potato. These are not the villains they were previously held to be, but provide vitamins and fibre essential to a healthy diet. They are also filling, which is why you will not feel so hungry following the Inglewood Plan as you did when you dieted previously.

To sum up, what matters is the amount of food you eat and of that food, you should eat more fibre and less fat. So, cut yourself thicker slices of wholemeal bread, spread your low-fat spread more thinly and serve your jacket baked potato with yoghurt instead of butter!

FADS, FETISHES AND FASTING

Having established a sensible balanced way of eating, let's explode some of the sillier notions about slimming. More rubbish is written about dieting, I believe, than any other subject. The silliest has to be a book by a French doctor which advocates four glasses of Burgundy a day for obesity and a daily bottle of rosé wine for major obesity! And there is also a multi-million pound industry which makes a fortune out of people's gullibility and desire to lose weight fast. It takes time to lose weight and there are no short-cuts or miracle cures. The combination of exercise and a balanced way of calorie-counted eating is the only way. But other notions prevail.

First of all there are fad diets. These are as seasonal as Paris fashions and often extol the virtues of some 'wonder' food such as grapefruit or honey. You lose weight on these diets because your calorie intake is limited to less than 1,000 calories but, because nobody wants to live continually on a diet of bananas and milk or boiled eggs, you soon tire of this diet, go back to your old way of eating and put on all the weight you lost. Sometimes these diets put forward such unscientific claims as: 'you must never mix protein and carbohydrate' (I don't know what they think bread is!), or 'you should eat only protein-rich foods one day and only pineapples the next'. I am sure you are far too sensible to be taken in by this sort of nonsense!

I am not happy about the use of drugs such as appetite suppressants to aid weight loss except in very special circumstances when it is medically advisable. There are also aids on the market, sold without prescription, that advertise their efficiency as appetite suppressants. These work either as starch blockers, contain a bulking agent or are simply sugar. The starch blockers claim to reduce the absorption of starch but, while they work beautifully in a test tube, it seems that in the body they have little or no effect. The bulking agents – bran or cellulose – do not actually contain

Checking progress on the exercise bike

Jogging must be carefully regulated and the choice of footwear is vitally important

enough bulk to have any effect, and if they did you would feel thoroughly uncomfortable. You would be better off saving your money and eating a few sticks of celery or an apple to take the edge off your appetite. The appetite suppressants, which are basically sugar, do work for the moment – at the cost of a few calories – because they raise your blood sugar; but when the temporary effect wears off you will feel even hungrier than before.

Other aids include lecithin, kelp, cider vinegar (makes a great salad dressing but contains no magic powers) and various combinations of herbs. Many of these have a laxative or diuretic effect. Weight loss this way, I'm afraid is, if taken in small quantities, irrelevant and, if taken in any larger doses, frankly dangerous. All I can say about the magic qualities of seaweed and the like – though there are people who have quite a fetish about its slimming potential – is that it has never been scientifically proved to be of benefit. If it could help you slim I am quite certain that the drug companies would have isolated its magic property and made a fortune selling it by now.

Fasting is something quite different and many people come to Inglewood expecting to fast. The trouble with a short-term fast is that over four or five days you first burn off body sugar and then the lean muscle tissue leaving the fat untouched. To actually burn off the fat you would need to fast for a week to ten days and this should never be attempted except under strict medical supervision. And personally, here at Inglewood, I don't recommend it. After all, it does nothing to change your eating pattern and when you go home you will probably put the weight on again very quickly. So it seems a lot of trouble for nothing. I believe in educating people to change to a permanent balanced way of eating that will bring them to their ideal weight and maintain them there. This is what Inglewood and this book is all about.

STRESS, DEPRESSION AND LONELINESS

However good the eating plan, it will not have any effect if you still cannot control the way you eat. First of all, you are not alone. There are thousands of people who, though in control of other aspects of their life, cannot control the way they eat. Food dominates their life and they swing from dieting to compulsive eating with an ever-increasing sense of guilt.

In acute cases this will require personal medical help, but in many instances, it is simply a question of breaking through the vicious circle. You are depressed so you eat something 'comforting' to cheer yourself up and you then feel guilty and more depressed and so on. As you get fatter you have less energy and so you sit more and get even fatter. It's no fun at all and it is a situation that the author of this book knew all too well. Her situation was typical, a combination of depression and boredom which increased as she got fatter. Once she broke the pattern – which happened when she first came to

Inglewood – she steadily lost weight and gained more energy and her depression disappeared. I don't think that she now has the time to feel bored.

So, what you must do is find a way to break that boredom/depression barrier. The magic word is 'exercise'. It doesn't have to be violent – indeed it shouldn't be – but just getting on to your feet and going for a walk will help. Do a bit of gardening or, if you haven't got a garden, offer to weed a friend's. You will feel better physically, not to mention the satisfaction of looking at the tidy patch of garden, and you will certainly be popular with your friend! Anything is fine just as long as it gets you out of that chair and busy. The busier you are the less depressed you will feel and you won't have time to feel lonely.

Stress is another emotional trigger that can cause you to put on weight. Contrary to popular opinion, worry does not necessarily make you thin; in fact stress raises the level of fat in your blood. First of all, look at yourself and see whether you do eat under stress. Do you find yourself in the kitchen after a row with a slice of buttered bread in your mouth? Do you head for the refrigerator when you are criticised? Do you pick up a chocolate bar in the supermarket when everything has gone wrong and it's crowded and everybody keeps hitting you with their trolleys? You are not alone.

Once you have recognised the danger areas, you must prepare for them. Amnesiac eating which you do not enjoy – and you never do enjoy the food you stuff down so hurriedly when anxious or angry – is a pointless exercise. So find another outlet. Buy yourself a large cushion and kick it when you are angry, if that helps. If you find yourself in the kitchen, make yourself a cup of tea or coffee and take it straight out of the kitchen, away from temptation. When you are feeling anxious, find alternative ways of comforting yourself. Enjoy a long bath, for example, or lie back and listen to your favourite piece of music. Do something selfish for yourself. Pamper yourself, you deserve it.

If you do not agree with that last sentence then it's time to look at your self-image. Here at Inglewood all the staff combine to make you feel good, but let me tell you that you are much more worthwhile and attractive than you think you are. If you don't believe me, make a list of your good qualities. These can be as simple as 'I'm tidy' and 'I answer letters promptly' to 'I am a kind mother' and 'I have a warm smile'. Write them all down. You'll find the list is much longer than you thought. You'll see that you are not nearly as awful as you thought!

Sometimes my patients tell me how dreadful they are because they fall by the wayside and cannot keep to a diet. 'Forget diets,' I tell them. 'Follow this plan, and if you have a lapse and eat all the foods you should avoid, that is all it is – a lapse.' You will find this repeated in the menu plans; it is not the end of your slimming, nor the world, if you have a bottle of wine or a slice of chocolate cake – in fact a lot of alcohol will often lead to a weakening in your resolve and you eating all the wrong things. You are human, that's all. Tomorrow is another day and you will go back to your pattern of healthy eating. You don't need to punish yourself or feel guilty. Don't dwell on it but I hope you enjoyed it. Yes, enjoyed it. After all, what is it but an occasional indulgence which you should enjoy to the full. Just try not to do it too often.

The word enjoyment crops up throughout this book. Enjoying good nutritious food means you won't want to change back to your previous way of eating; enjoying the exercise you choose means that you won't want to give it up; enjoying life means that you you have beaten the bugbears of depression and loneliness and haven't got the time to let food dominate your life.

The Inglewood Plan liberates you from being a slave to a diet and allows you to lead your life to the full as the slim, fit person you have always wanted to be.

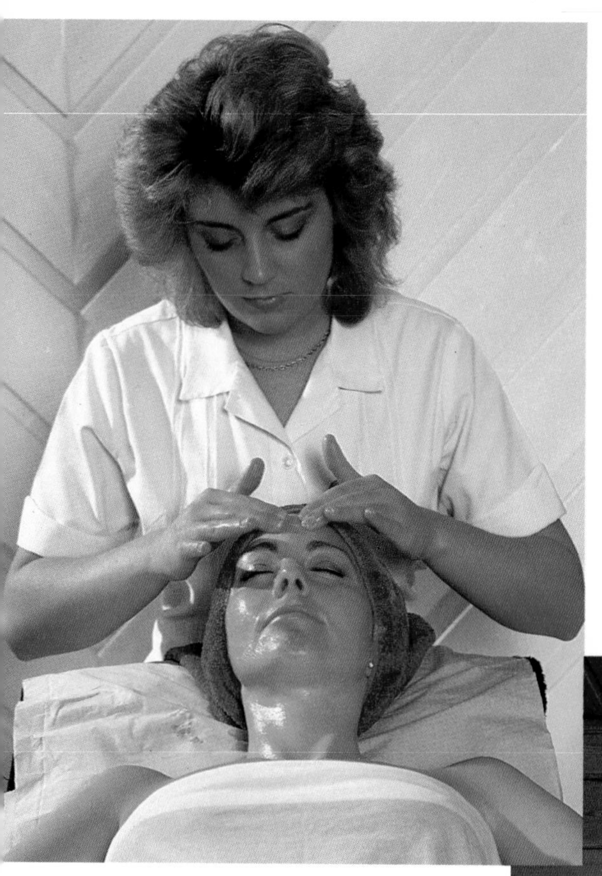

A guest enjoying one of Inglewood's beauty treatments

Sit back and relax in a steamy sauna

TABLE A

WOMEN

Height	*Acceptable average*	*Acceptable*	*Obese*
ft in	st lb	st lb	st lb
4 10	7 4	6 8 – 8 7	10 3
4 11	7 6	6 10 – 8 10	10 6
5 0	7 9	6 12 – 8 13	10 10
5 1	7 12	7 1 – 9 2	10 13
5 2	8 1	7 4 – 9 5	11 3
5 3	8 4	7 7 – 9 8	11 7
5 4	8 8	7 10 – 9 12	11 12
5 5	8 11	7 13 – 10 2	12 2
5 6	9 2	8 2 – 10 6	12 7
5 7	9 6	8 6 – 10 10	12 12
5 8	9 10	8 10 – 11 0	13 3
5 9	10 0	9 0 – 11 4	13 8
5 10	10 4	9 4 – 11 9	14 0
5 11	10 8	9 8 – 12 0	14 6
6 0	10 12	9 12 – 12 5	14 12

MEN

Height	*Acceptable average*	*Acceptable*	*Obese*
ft in	st lb	st lb	st lb
5 2	8 9	8 0 – 10 1	12 1
5 3	9 1	8 3 – 10 4	12 5
5 4	9 4	8 6 – 10 8	12 10
5 5	9 7	8 9 – 10 12	13 0
5 6	9 10	8 12 – 11 2	13 5
5 7	10 0	9 2 – 11 7	13 11
5 8	10 5	9 6 – 11 12	14 3
5 9	10 9	9 10 – 12 2	14 8
5 10	10 13	10 0 – 12 6	14 13
5 11	11 4	10 4 – 12 11	15 5
6 0	11 8	10 8 – 13 2	15 11
6 1	11 12	10 12 – 13 7	16 3
6 2	12 3	11 2 – 13 12	16 9
6 3	12 8	11 6 – 14 3	17 1
6 4	12 13	11 10 – 14 8	17 7

WOMEN

Height	*Acceptable average*	*Acceptable*	*Obese*
metres	kg	kg	kg
1.45	46.0	42 – 53	64
1.48	46.5	42 – 54	65
1.50	47.0	43 – 55	66
1.52	48.5	44 – 57	68
1.54	49.5	44 – 58	69
1.56	50.4	45 – 58	70
1.58	51.3	46 – 59	71
1.60	52.6	48 – 61	73
1.62	54.0	49 – 62	74
1.64	55.4	50 – 64	77
1.66	56.8	51 – 65	78
1.68	58.1	52 – 66	79
1.70	60.0	53 – 67	80
1.72	61.3	55 – 69	83
1.75	62.6	56 – 70	84
1.76	64.0	58 – 72	86
1.78	65.3	59 – 74	89

MEN

Height	*Acceptable average*	*Acceptable*	*Obese*
metres	kg	kg	kg
1.58	55.8	51 – 64	77
1.60	57.6	52 – 65	78
1.62	58.6	53 – 66	79
1.64	59.6	54 – 67	80
1.66	60.6	55 – 69	83
1.68	61.7	56 – 71	85
1.70	63.5	58 – 73	88
1.72	65.0	59 – 74	89
1.74	66.5	60 – 75	90
1.76	68.0	62 – 77	92
1.78	69.4	64 – 79	95
1.80	71.0	65 – 80	96
1.82	72.6	66 – 82	98
1.84	74.2	67 – 84	101
1.86	75.8	69 – 86	103
1.88	77.6	71 – 88	106
1.90	79.3	73 – 90	108
1.92	81.0	75 – 93	112

·Individual·Plans·for· Individual·Lifestyles·

Patricia Graham and Antoinette Moses

As you have read, the Inglewood Plan is not a diet but a way of life. Eating a healthy balanced diet should come naturally after a while but for those who prefer some guidance we have mapped out a few sample weeks. If you follow these you will lose weight steadily and using the other calorie-counted recipes in this book, you will be able to chop and change as it suits you. They have been written to fit in as much as possible with the lifestyle you have, whether it is at home or constantly out and about. And there is also a special section for vegetarian slimmers.

SHOPPING

This is an important area and often forgotten. When you are trying to lose weight it is important to make a list and only buy what you need. Otherwise you may buy much more and once it is at home you will eat it. If the number of people in your house has decreased – the children have gone, for example – then make sure the amount of food you buy goes down in proportion. Buy only what you need and never buy biscuits or cakes or sweets thinking that your husband or your children will eat them. Once they are home you will eat them too, and none of these things are healthy for anyone, so buy a healthy alternative. Some extra fruit perhaps; maybe use the money you have saved on the biscuits for something unusual like melon out of season. Indulge in healthy luxuries and you won't want unhealthy foods any more.

GENERAL NOTES TO THE PLANS

Each plan has its own notes, but as a general rule you should remember that you have a daily allowance of skimmed milk and low-fat spread in addition to the other foods listed. There is no point just switching to skimmed milk if you do not change the other elements of your diet, but as part of a general change to healthier eating it makes sense not to waste calories on full-fat milk or butter. And you may well find that after a bit you prefer skimmed milk. You can still use butter on occasions; nobody would ask you to eat asparagus without butter, but it's a very short season, so make it an occasional treat. But if you are in any way susceptible to heart disease then try to cut it out altogether.

These plans are meant to be flexible so switch as much as you like, providing you don't go over the calories you are allotted. You will find a basic calorie guide in Appendix 1. Once you have reached your target, then you can just add extra staples such as fruit, vegetables, bread and potatoes to give you the right calorie intake to maintain your new slim shape.

MICROWAVE COOKING

Guests at Inglewood often ask whether they can have special recipes for microwave cooking. In fact, you hardly need a special book provided you follow the manufacturer's instructions and adapt our recipes accordingly. So many things can be cooked in a microwave and more quickly. A baked potato takes five minutes, a casserole forty-five minutes and a roast chicken can be cooked in half an hour. Just remember, never put any metal container in your microwave oven, and all food completely enclosed in skin, such as baked potato or fish, must be thoroughly pricked or slashed, otherwise it will burst and splatter all over your oven. Food in a microwave oven must be covered with special microwave clingfilm greaseproof paper secured with cocktail sticks. Because microwave ovens cook so quickly you will find yourself spending less time in the kitchen, which is always good news to slimmers, and with a little bit of practice you'll find most recipes in this book can be adapted for a microwave oven.

The·Inglewood· FAMILY·LIFESTYLE·PLAN

This plan is aimed at those at home, particularly women with small children. These menus allow for a balanced day's eating with a substantial dinner you can enjoy with the rest of your family. Ingredients in the plan are per person, so just multiply by the number of mouths you have to feed and whether or not the rest of your family are trying to lose weight. If they are slim or you have active teenagers you can increase their portions.

When you are at home all day there are temptations around you constantly and it is easy to nibble. If that is your problem, you may prefer to follow 'The Inglewood Little and Often Diet' (see p30). Otherwise make yourself a big bowl of prepared raw vegetables such as carrots, green peppers, celery, cucumber and cauliflower florets and nibble from this when the urge comes over you. Also, note your danger times. If you are busy at breakfast-time getting everyone out of the house and do not get hungry until lunch-time, but cannot resist eating something when the children have their tea, then skip breakfast or part of it and eat your slice of toast or even your cereal at tea-time. This won't hurt you and you will, incidentally, be less likely to over-indulge in the evening. Whereas if you simply sip your tea, gnawed by hunger while your children nosh beans on toast, you may well feel deprived and eat too much either while preparing dinner or at dinner-time itself. The aim of the Inglewood Way is to find a lifetime pattern of eating that suits you. After all, if you don't feel happy you won't keep it up. We all know that to get slim and fit and stay so, you have to find a balanced plan of eating that suits your life and allows for your weaknesses. That is why we make our menu plans as flexible as possible.

THE PLAN

The following plan is a strict 1,000 calorie menu for consistent fast weight loss. If you are very active, you can add another 250–500 calories a day and still lose. When you reach your ideal weight, keep to the same pattern but increase your calories from 1750 to 2000. You should do this by increasing the amount of unrefined carbohydrates you eat, such as eating a larger jacket potato, an extra slice of wholemeal bread, more brown rice, etc. Also feel free to increase the amount of vegetables, salad and fruit you eat, but don't increase your fat intake. The low-fat spread and milk allowance, as well as the oil used in recipes, is quite adequate. And you don't need any more protein than what is allowed here either. The 4oz/113g of meat or 6oz/170g of fish as well as cheese, eggs and beans is quite enough. Don't forget you get a lot of protein from staples such as bread and potatoes.

Daily Allowance
½pt/300ml skimmed milk
½oz/14g low-fat spread

BREAKFASTS

These are interchangeable. They are all around 200 calories so feel free to chop and change.

(a) ½ grapefruit
2oz/56g All Bran with chopped apple
milk from allowance
tea or coffee with milk from allowance

(b) 4 fl oz/113ml natural fruit juice
1 slice wholemeal toast from large loaf
1 rasher back bacon well grilled
tea or coffee with milk from allowance

(c) ½ grapefruit
1½oz/42g muesli with small chopped apple
milk from allowance

(d) 1 orange
1 × 5.3oz/150g can baked beans
1 slice wholemeal bread from small loaf with spread from allowance

(e) slice of melon
1 boiled egg
1 slice wholemeal bread from large loaf with Marmite if desired
tea or coffee with milk from allowance

(f) ½ grapefruit
2 slices wholemeal bread from large loaf (toasted if desired) with spread from allowance
1 level tbsp/15ml jam or marmalade

(g) ½ grapefruit
1oz/28g All Bran with milk from allowance
1 slice wholemeal bread from large loaf (toasted if desired) with spread from allowance and Marmite, if liked

LUNCHES AND DINNERS

Monday

LUNCH
Any low-calorie soup
2 crispbreads with spread from allowance
1 piece of fruit

DINNER
Cold meat (from yesterday's joint or lean ham), allow 4oz/113g per person
6oz/170g baked jacket potato
salad with low calorie dressing
fresh fruit salad (no added sugar)

Tuesday

LUNCH
1 × 5.3oz/150g can sugar-reduced baked beans in tomato sauce
1 slice wholemeal bread from large loaf with ¼oz/7g low-fat spread
1 piece of fruit

DINNER
6oz/170g Fish Kebabs (p58)
4oz/113g boiled new potatoes with spread from allowance
green vegetables (no extra spread or butter)
Home-made Fruit Yogurt:
1 × 5.3oz/150g carton natural yogurt mixed with 2ox/56g fresh or frozen blackberries/strawberries or whatever you prefer, or use a can of fruit packed with fruit juice, not syrup. Drain all but 1tbsp/15ml of the juice and mix with the yogurt.

Wednesday

LUNCH *Cottage Cheese Salad*
2oz/50g cottage cheese
1oz/7g sweetcorn
1 orange peeled and chopped
½ small chopped green pepper

Mix together.

DINNER *Italian Sautéed Lamb's Liver*
4oz/113g lamb's liver (per person)
1tbsp/15ml sunflower margarine
1tsp/5ml crumbled dry sage

Cut liver into thick slices and sauté each side for about 4 minutes in the sunflower margarine and crumbled sage. Serve immediately with spinach (no added butter or spread) and puréed potatoes using skimmed milk and spread from allowance.
1 piece of fruit

Thursday

LUNCH
1 × 4oz/113g baked potato
1oz/28g grated Edam
1 piece of fruit

DINNER
Spaghetti Bolognese (p82)
green salad (dressed with lemon juice and chopped herbs only)
½ × 5.3oz/150g carton natural yogurt with 1 small chopped apple (dusted with cinnamon if liked)

Friday

LUNCH *Pasta and Chicken Salad*
1oz/28g pasta shells (weighed dry)
½ green pepper
4oz/113g cooked chicken (no skin)
2 tomatoes

Boil the pasta until it is *al dente*, rinse under a cold tap and allow to cool. Chop the chicken, and mix with the chopped pepper and tomatoes with the pasta shells. Season with plenty of fresh-ground black pepper. Serve with Tomato Dressing (p115).

DINNER
Fish Pie (p58)
1 piece of fruit

Saturday

LUNCH
Greek Salad (p45)
1 piece of fruit

DINNER
Chicken in White Wine (p65)
1oz/28g (weighed dry) long grain rice per person
Blackberry Sorbet (p104)

Sunday

LUNCH
Roast lamb (allow 4oz/113g per person)
6oz/175g baked jacket potato
Rhubarb and Orange Compôte (p109)

DINNER
French Onion Soup (p52) (with 1 slice wholemeal bread from large loaf)
1 piece of fruit

The·Inglewood· BUSINESSMAN'S·MENU·PLAN

As a busy executive with a lifestyle which includes business eating as well as a full social life it is very easy to gradually put on weight. And that added weight plus the stress of your work puts a lot of strain on your heart. Getting down to your right weight will not only make you healthier, it will also make you better at your job. You will have more energy and even find that your head is clearer when it comes to making decisions.

In addition to following a better diet it is important to do some exercise every day. A strenuous workout playing squash once a week is not sensible: it is more likely to cause a heart attack. So turn to our chapter on exercise and promise your body a few minutes every day, even if it is just our warm-up programme.

If you eat a lot during the day you may be tempted to skip breakfast or even keep going until dinner with nothing but coffee. This will not help you to lose weight. It is better to have a light breakfast and eat less at each meal. A very heavy late dinner just before you collapse in front of the television and go to bed will not be burned up as fast as a heavy lunch. So if you do go to regular dinner parties, do not over-indulge too often.

As a man you will probably lose weight fast on 1500–2000 calories a day and can maintain your weight on 2700–2900 calories a day. The following diet is therefore based on 1500–1750 calories and once you have reached your target weight you can add to it with discretion using your good sense and our calorie guide in Appendix 1. This menu plan is also low in cholesterol, so even when you reach your target weight it makes sense for you – and your heart – to stay on a low-cholesterol diet.

Daily Allowance
1pt/500ml skimmed milk
1oz/28g low-fat spread

BREAKFASTS

With a busy routine you probably prefer to stick to the same breakfast every morning with a change at weekends, so that is what we offer.

Monday to Friday

THE CEREAL BREAKFAST
½ grapefruit
2oz/56g All Bran with 1 apple chopped and 1tbsp/15ml raisins
milk from allowance
tea or coffee with milk from allowance

or

THE TOAST BREAKFAST
½ grapefruit
2 slices wholemeal bread or toast with low-calorie spread from allowance and Marmite if wished
tea or coffee with milk from allowance

Saturday
½ grapefruit
1 egg poached or boiled
grilled mushrooms and tomatoes
1 slice wholemeal bread with spread from allowance
tea or coffee with milk from allowance

Sunday
1 slice melon
2oz/56g muesli with ½ chopped banana and milk from allowance
tea or coffee with milk from allowance

LUNCHES

Monday to Friday

EATING OUT
This is the hardest to calculate and it is very easy to eat and drink a few hundred extra calories without noticing it. Drinks in particular are dangerous, giving you empty calories, ie all the fuel to make fat with none of the nutrients. Today, luckily there is much less pressure to drink a lot of wine at a business lunch. Many executives have switched to Perrier and it certainly makes it easier to work in the afternoon. And if you're driving you have every reason not to drink alcohol. If you are having a pub lunch try and keep the beer to ½pt. Two pints of Guinness, for example, comes out at close on 400 calories – your entire lunchtime allowance. So watch what you drink.

While you can keep a packed lunch to within 350 to 400 calories without difficulty, you can hardly spend your meal out totting up the calories with a calculator, so here are a few basic guidelines.

STARTER
Go for fruit. Melon or grapefruit is the lowest-

calorie way to start a meal. A skinny piece of Parma ham with your melon won't hurt you either. Consommé is also a good starter either hot or cold but beware of thick soups as they may contain cream and should be avoided. Seafood is safe, though eat it in moderation, as long as you eschew the mayonnaise. Mussels are very low in calories, as are smoked salmon and oysters. Smoked trout is another sensible choice, as long as you don't put butter on your accompanying bread. Mackerel is a much fattier fish and not such a good idea except as a main course.

MAIN DISH

Go for grilled food. A plain grilled fish or steak is the most sensible choice. Braised kidneys or calves' liver is also good and most Italian restaurants do the last with sage (*Fegato alla salvia*), but make sure that you ask for the accompanying vegetables to be served without butter. It's better for your heart quite apart from your waistline. An omelette is usually fairly low, as is a salad if it's not swamped with mayonnaise. But if you are following a low-calorie diet try not to have more than three egg yolks a week. Avoid meat in heavy sauces, made-up dishes such as lasagne (yes, you can make a slimming version at home but the chef probably uses lots of oil, butter and cheese as well as the pasta). Avoid anything with cream or anything fried. You still have plenty of choice and you are less likely to get post-prandial indigestion.

DESSERT

If you are happy with coffee, fine. Otherwise steer towards fruit. Either fresh fruit in season or a fresh fruit salad – without cream, of course. Fruit sorbets are generally safe, as is crème caramel and even, for a treat, Zabaglione (p110) if you are lunching all'Italiano. It is not likely to be more than 200 calories, while apple pie and cream could go over your 400 mark, and as for chocolate cake with cream, it's not what your heart would choose and it's not fair to burden yourself with so many empty calories.

To sum up: if you eat out very often then it obviously makes sense to head for the lightest kind of lunch. Grilled fish with green vegetables and a fresh fruit salad. If it is a special occasion then you can relax more without going for the heaviest dishes. And try to have a light supper in the evening. The aim is to enjoy your meal and leave feeling satisfied rather than stuffed.

PACKED LUNCHES

This does not mean that you have to eat the plain yogurt and apple your secretary brings to work. These lunches are aimed at being satisfying without being heavy. They offer a balanced midday cold meal and will not take long to prepare. In fact you – or your wife – can make them all in a batch at the beginning of the week and freeze them in packets. You just take out one packet each day.

Each of these packed lunches is about 350 calories which should satisfy you, but leave you plenty of calories for your main meal in the evening. You obviously don't have to stick to the days as given.

Monday

2 × 6oz/170g roast chicken legs (raw weight, skin removed)
crisp lettuce heart
1 piece of fruit

Tuesday

Camembert Salad

3oz/85g Camembert, cubed
1 pear
3 sticks celery
5 halves of walnuts

Mix the ingredients together and place in an airtight container on a bed of lettuce.

Wednesday

Tuna Pâté (p28) (one portion)
2 × 1½oz/42g slices wholemeal bread
1 piece of fruit

Thursday

Ham and Lettuce Rolls

4oz/113g ham
large lettuce leaves

Lay large lettuce leaves on a plate and cover each one with a slice of ham, roll up and secure with a cocktail stick.

Wholemeal roll with low-calorie spread from allowance
1 piece of fruit

Friday

Smoked Salmon Sandwiches

4 slices wholemeal bread (from a small loaf)
2oz/56g smoked salmon

Spread the bread with low-calorie spread from

allowance and fill with smoke salmon which you have sprinkled with lemon juice. Pack in foil.

2 tomatoes
1 piece of fruit

DINNERS

In these dinners, which are, of course only suggestions, I have tried to give you low-cholesterol substitutes to meat on many days. If you have roast chicken or turkey for Sunday lunch instead of roast beef this is even better. You can switch days with these menus or use other dishes from our plentiful supply of recipes. This way there is no danger of becoming bored with what you eat and heading back into bad habits. If you have to drink alcohol with your meals I suggest that you try and limit wine to two or three times a week instead of every day. Naturally, if you have people over you will want to drink wine, but make sure you have a bottle of mineral water on the table as well so that you can quench your thirst with water and thus cut back on the amount you drink. And if you do drink a lot one evening, try to cut out the alcohol for the next couple of days. It's worth it for the sake of your heart as well as your waistline.

Monday
cold meat (left over from Sunday lunch or 4oz/113g lean ham)
Fennel Salad (p92)
Grape and Celery Salad (p93)
baked jacket potato with spread from allowance
Baked Apples with Dates (p104)

Tuesday
Salmon Baked in Foil (p61)
boiled new potatoes with spread from allowance and mint
broccoli
Fresh Fruit Salad (no added sugar) (p106)

Wednesday
grilled chicken pieces (remove skin)
grilled tomatoes and mushrooms
baked jacket potato
1 piece of fruit

Thursday
Trout in Orange Sauce (p62)
puréed potatoes (mashed with skimmed milk and spread from allowance)
4oz/113g peas
Rhubarb and Orange Compôte (p109)

Friday
Mushroom Soufflé (p85)
green salad
1 piece of fruit

WEEKEND MEALS

Saturday

BRUNCH
½ grapefruit
1½oz/42g muesli with 1 chopped apple, ½ chopped banana and milk from allowance
2 rashers grilled back bacon
2oz/56g grilled mushrooms
1 grilled tomato
2 slices wholemeal bread from small loaf (toasted if wished) with spread from allowance and 1tsp/5ml marmalade
tea or coffee with spread from allowance

TEATIME
1 plain biscuit
1 piece of fruit
tea or coffee with milk from allowance

DINNER PARTY
Cold Watercress Soup (p51)
Pigeons with Grapes (p68)
baked potatoes with yogurt
Courgette Salad (p92)
Pineapple with Port (p109)

Sunday

BREAKFAST
2 slices wholemeal bread (toasted if wished) with spread from allowance and 1 level tbsp/15ml jam or marmalade
tea or coffee with milk from allowance

LUNCH
roast beef (allow 4oz/113g per person)
8oz/226g jacket potato with spread from allowance
green vegetables, as much as you like but no added spread or butter
Banana Cheese (p104)

SUPPER
Potato, Onion and Celery Soup (p53)
1 wholemeal roll
1 piece of fruit

The·Inglewood· BUSINESSWOMAN'S·MENU·PLAN

FAMILY BUSINESSWOMAN

The reason that I have treated the businessman and the businesswoman separately and not written one single businessperson's low-calorie week of menus is that their calorific needs are different, as are their eating patterns. This is particularly true of the single career woman to whom I shall return.

But firstly, what about the married businesswoman, holding down a job and looking after a family? It can be particularly difficult for you to lose weight, but if you want to lose weight quickly and steadily I suggest a daily average plan of 1,000–1,200 calories. Once you have reached your target weight this can rise to 1,500–2,000.

Also, however busy you are, I would stress the need for you to get some regular exercise every day, even if it is just walking to work or part of the way to work. Just getting off the bus or the underground one stop before your destination and walking the rest of the way can make all the difference. Even this small amount of regular exercise can gradually make you feel fitter, brighter and much better able to cope with your work load.

You probably prefer to have your main meal in the evening with your family and may be too busy during the day to worry much about food. My suggestion is that you follow the following Businesswoman's Breakfast and Lunch Plan which gives you 150 calorie breakfasts and 200 calorie lunches and then switch over to the Businessman's dinner menus as you may well be cooking these anyway to slim your spouse. You should also allow yourself ½pt/300ml skimmed milk every day plus ½oz/14g low-fat spread.

Watch for your danger hour, it is probably when – as mine was when I worked in an office – the hunger pangs attack you while you are preparing dinner. There's no point in my saying wait until dinner, you must prepare for these moments of crisis. In this case I suggest a bowl of ready-prepared raw vegetables such as sticks of cucumber and carrot. These can be dipped in garlic salt if you like, for a salty nibble that satisfies those pangs but doesn't destroy your diet plan like nuts or (my own ogre) slivers of cheese would. If you take the edge off your appetite like this you'll also be less in danger of overloading your plate with extra calories at dinner.

SINGLE CAREER WOMAN

The lifestyle of the career woman is often different. Again, you may prefer to eat less during the day and even skip breakfast. It is allowed and is not nearly as sinful as some dieticians used to say. In this case, you will have calories in hand for your evening meal, which you may often take out. Dining out presents the same problems as lunching out and you should read the general guidelines for eating out in the Businessman's section (p24). If you only go out once a week there is no harm in having a really low-calorie day prior to going out and then enjoying yourself when you do go out. But try not to go mad and choose profiteroles with whipped cream and chocolate which can easily contain your whole day's allowance of 1,000 calories. But otherwise, you can relax. There is no harm in totting up your calories over two days and if this does not exceed 2,000 calories you will continue to lose weight. However, don't do this too often, certainly no more than once a week.

You will notice that I said prior to going out. If you say to yourself, 'I'll have a good day tomorrow', the chances are high that you won't. There are many reasons. Firstly, your blood sugar may be low from drinking alcohol over your dinner which will make you crave more food; secondly, it's easy to think, 'I've blown it anyway, so what harm will a bit more do'; thirdly, you will have broken your low-calorie routine and it's hard enough to go back to your usual regimen, but much harder to have a really low-calorie day. So, prepare in advance, but don't have less than 300 calories. Nevertheless, if you don't manage this advance preparation do not act as if this is the end of your dieting or the world. Remember this is not a crash diet, it is a plan for life. Tomorrow is another day, so start again. It may take you a day longer to reach your target but that is not so dreadful, is it? Guilt over one night's indulgence can lead into a whole cycle of bingeing and remorse which is bad for your body, your morale and you. So, however erratic your lifestyle, if you follow the basic principles of the Inglewood way of eating plus take some regular daily exercise, you will lose weight and stay slim.

Daily Allowance
½pt/300ml of skimmed milk
½oz/14g low-fat spread

BREAKFASTS

(a) 1½oz/42g All Bran with 1 medium chopped apple
tea or coffee with milk from allowance

(b) ½ grapefruit
2 slices wholemeal bread from small loaf with spread from allowance, Marmite if wished
tea or coffee with milk from allowance

(c) 1 boiled or poached egg
1 slice of wholemeal bread from small loaf, toasted if wished with spread from allowance
tea or coffee with milk from allowance

(d) 1 medium orange
2 slices of wholemeal bread from small loaf with spread from allowance and Marmite if wished
tea or coffee with milk from allowance

(e) 1oz/28g cornflakes with 2 level tbsp/30ml sultanas
tea or coffee with milk from allowance

(f) 1oz/28g muesli with 2tbsp/30ml natural yogurt
tea or coffee with milk from allowance

(g) 1oz/28g All Bran with 1 medium chopped banana
tea or coffee with milk from allowance

(h) 1 × 5.3oz/150g carton natural yogurt with 2tbsp/30ml Jordan's Original Crunchy
tea or coffee with milk from allowance

LUNCHES

(a) TUNA PATE
3½oz/100g tuna in brine
1oz/28g low-fat soft cheese
1tbsp/15ml tomato puree

Mix well together and pile on to Ryvita or serve as a dip with your Ryvita and sticks of sliced green pepper, celery and cucumber.

(b) SANDWICHES
2 slices wholemeal bread from small loaf with one of the following.
(i) *Egg*: Scramble 1 egg with 2tbsp/30ml skimmed milk in a non-stick pan and add 1tbsp/15ml cress. Season to taste and spread.

(ii) *Ham*: 2oz/56g of lean ham (all fat removed) with made-up mustard if liked.

(iii) *Cheese and Apple*: 1½oz/42g low-fat soft cheese with 1 medium apple cut into slices. Dust with cinnamon if liked.

(iv) *Beef*: 2oz/56g of lean roast beef and a few crisp lettuce leaves. Add made-up mustard or horse-radish if liked.

(v) *Greek*: Take 1½oz/42g feta cheese, 2 tomatoes, sliced, and two olives with the stones removed.

(vi) *Crab*: Take 3oz/85g crabmeat and mix with 1tbsp/15ml natural yogurt and 1tsp/5ml tomato purée.

(vii) *Smoked Salmon*: Take 2oz/56g smoked salmon and sprinkle with lemon juice.

(viii) *Cottage Cheese*: Take 3oz/85g cottage cheese and mix with fresh chopped chives or sliced green and red peppers or chopped celery or 1tsp/5ml sweetcorn.

(ix) *Italian*: This is best as a toasted sandwich. Toast one side of the bread. Spread the other with 1oz/28g Mozzarella cheese and 1 tomato, sliced. Replace under the grill and toast until cheese melts. If you have any fresh basil, add ½tsp/2.5ml of this as well or a ¼tsp/1.25ml of Italian dried herbs.

(x) *Cheese and Pickle*: Take 2oz/56g low-fat soft cheese and add 1tbsp/15ml any sweet pickle or chutney.

The·Inglewood· VEGETARIAN'S·SLIMFAST·MENU

If you are a vegetarian, then it is easy to put on weight by eating too much of a good thing – too many wholemeal honey cakes and oat biscuits. These you will have to cut down on until you reach your target weight and then indulge in moderation. You may also be getting too much of your protein from milk and cheese which gives you too much cholesterol in your diet. Therefore you should make sure you eat enough protein-giving pulses and get plenty of iron from beans and dark green vegetables. Dried fruits are also iron-rich and will alleviate your sweet-tooth cravings, if you have any.

The week's menu is not rigid. You can switch it from day to day and use it as a guide. It is based on a strict 1,000 calories a day, so that if you are taking a lot of exercise you can add an additional 500 calories. A male can certainly lose weight on 1,500 calories a day and a young man taking plenty of exercise will need at least 2,000 calories a day. So, add to these menus according to your family needs and using the calorie guide in the appendix. It makes good dietary sense to add to your protein and starch allowances rather than eat any more fat. More cereal, more potato or wholewheat pasta can certainly be added according to your body's needs; it is up to you to keep within that limit.

Daily Allowance

1pt/300ml skimmed milk or ½pt/150ml silver top milk
½oz/14g Flora or other vegetable margarine *or*
1oz/28g low-fat spread

You can drink as much tea or coffee with milk from your allowance as you like, and slimline drinks and Perrier or hot Marmite with water.

DAILY MENUS

Monday

BREAKFAST
1½oz/42g muesli with milk from allowance with 1tbsp/15ml flaked almonds and 4 chopped dried apricots
tea or coffee with milk from allowance

LUNCH
3tbsp/45ml cooked brown rice with slimmer's Ratatouille (p86)
4oz/113g natural yogurt with ½ medium banana, sliced

DINNER
2oz/56g Roquefort with 1 pear, sliced and served with lettuce
2 Ryvita or other crispbread with spread from allowance

Tuesday

BREAKFAST
½ grapefruit
2 slices wholemeal toast from small loaf with spread from allowance and Marmite
tea or coffee with milk from allowance

LUNCH
Cottage Cheese and Melon Salad
Slice 5oz/140g melon with as much celery, cucumber and watercress as you wish and serve with 4oz/113g cottage cheese
2 digestive biscuits

DINNER
Chick Peas with Spinach and Potatoes (p80)
slice fresh pineapple with 1tsp/5ml sherry

Wednesday

BREAKFAST
½ grapefruit
1½oz/42g All Bran with 1 medium chopped apple
milk from allowance
tea or coffee with milk from allowance

LUNCH
1 × 5.3oz/150g can sugar-reduced baked beans on
1 slice wholemeal toast from a small loaf
1 piece of fruit

DINNER
Cauliflower Cheese (p85)
4oz/113g potato baked in its jacket with spread from allowance
1 piece of fruit *or*
4oz/113g natural yogurt with bran if liked

Thursday

BREAKFAST
1 slice melon
1oz/28g muesli with 1oz/28g dried peaches
milk from allowance
tea or coffee with milk from allowance

LUNCH
Lentil Salad (p94)
with Raita (yogurt with cucumber and fresh herbs) (p97)

DINNER
2oz/56g wholewheat pasta (weighed dry) with Tomato Sauce (p113) and 2tbsp/30ml grated parmesan
1 piece of fruit

Friday

BREAKFAST
½ grapefruit
1½oz/42g All Bran with milk from allowance
tea or coffee with milk from allowance

LUNCH
1 × 1½oz/42g slice wholemeal bread from large loaf with
2oz/56g low-fat soft cheese
1 medium sliced apple. Dust with cinnamon.
(This is ideal for a packed lunch)

DINNER
Beans with Aubergines and Mushrooms (p78)
1 slice wholemeal bread with spread from allowance
1 piece of fruit

Saturday

BREAKFAST
(Allowing for a dinner party)
1 × 5.3oz/150g can sugar-reduced baked beans on wholemeal toast from small loaf with spread from allowance
tea or coffee with milk from allowance

LUNCH
2 pieces of fruit

DINNER PARTY
Mushroom and Tarragon Soup (p53)
(*Note* Use the milk from your daily allowance)
Stuffed Courgettes (p89)
served with a bowl of yogurt which is mixed with onion rings and chopped cucumber
Pears Poached in Red Wine (p108)
1 glass dry white wine

Sunday

BREAKFAST
½ grapefruit
1 slice wholemeal toast with spread from allowance and Marmite
tea or coffee with milk from allowance

LUNCH
Curry lunch, serve together:

1 bowl Dahl (lentil purée) (p81)
Steamed Green Beans (p88)
Brown Rice with Cardamons and Nuts (5 nuts per person) (p80)
2 bananas, sliced
bowl of grated carrot in orange juice sprinkled with cumin seed
1 bowl Raita (p97)

DINNER
2 crispbreads with 4oz/113g cottage cheese
1 piece of fruit
hot milky drink with milk from allowance

The·Inglewood· LITTLE·AND·OFTEN·DIET

This diet is ideal for those at home, for the inveterate nibbler, for those living alone and for those who need an extra boost to their diet. Because these meals are spaced throughout the day it has been proved that the body burns up the food at a faster rate and weight loss on this diet is not only rapid but steady. This example is a strict 1,000 calorie diet though those who are doing a lot of exercise could allow themselves another 250 calories a day and men could live on an additional 500–750 calories a day.

The diet is very simple. There are three meals and three snacks. These should all be eaten in one 24-hour period, but leave 2 hours between each meal and snack. You can eat them in any order you like, but try not to eat the heaviest meal just before you go to bed.

While you will lose well on this diet, do not weigh yourself *more than twice a week*. Once a week 'spot check' on the size of your portions – they tend to increase with time! Cut back accordingly.

Daily Allowance

In addition to your six meals and snacks you should have each day ½pt/300ml skimmed milk and ½oz/14g low fat spread.

MEAL 1 BREAKFAST

Choose from one of these:

(a) ½ grapefruit
1½oz/42g All Bran with
1 small apple and milk from allowance
tea or coffee with milk from allowance

(b) ½ grapefruit
2 slices of wholemeal bread or toast from small loaf with spread from allowance and 1tsp/5ml Marmite
tea or coffee with milk from allowance

(c) 1 slice melon
1 slice wholemeal bread or toast with spread from allowance and 1tsp/5ml honey

(d) 1 slice wholemeal toast from small loaf with 4oz/113g baked beans
tea or coffee with milk from allowance

(e) 1oz/28g muesli and ½ small banana and 1 level tbsp/15ml sultanas and milk from allowance
tea or coffee with milk from allowance

(f) ½ grapefruit
1 slice wholemeal toast from small loaf with spread from allowance
1 egg (size 4) boiled or poached

SNACK 1

1 apple *or* 1 pear *or* 1 peach *or* 10 grapes *or* ½ medium banana

MEAL 2 LUNCH

Choose from one of these:

(a) 2oz/56g lean meat *or* 3oz/85g prawns
with green vegetables and spread from allowance
or green salad with 2tbsp/30ml Yogurt Dressing (p114)

(b) 1 egg poached *or* boiled
with green vegetables and spread from allowance
or green salad with 2tbsp/30ml Yogurt Dressing (p114)

(c) 1 × 4oz/113g jacket potato with 1tbsp/15ml grated Edam

(d) 1 × 4oz/113g jacket potato with 1tbsp/15ml cottage cheese with 1oz/28g prawns and chopped chives

(e) 4oz/113g cottage cheese (any variety)
1 tomato, celery and 2 slices extra-thin crispbread with spread from allowance

(f) 1 hardboiled egg with 1tbsp/15ml natural yogurt with 1 tomato and chopped celery to fill 1 × 5.3oz/150g cottage cheese carton
2 Ryvita with spread from allowance

(g) 2oz/56g lean chicken chopped with tomato and cucumber and 1tbsp/15ml yogurt and 1tsp/5ml made mustard to fill 1 × 5.3oz/150g cottage cheese carton
2 extra thin crispbreads with spread from allowance

(h) 2oz/56g ham chopped with 1tbsp/15ml green pepper and 1 tomato and 1tbsp/15ml natural yogurt in 1 × 5.3oz/150g cottage cheese carton
1 extra thin crispbread with spread from allowance

(i) 3oz/85g prawns with 2tbsp/30ml natural yogurt and 1tsp/5ml tomato purée and 1 tomato and shredded lettuce to fill 1 × 5.3oz/150g cottage cheese carton

SNACK 2

1 slice wholemeal bread from medium loaf with either 1oz/28g Edam
or 1oz/28g Brie
or 3oz/85g cottage cheese

MEAL 3 SUPPER

Choose from one of these:

(a) 3oz/85g ham
or 2 eggs
or 4oz/113g lean chicken without skin
or 3oz/85g poached salmon
or 4oz/113g steamed halibut
or 6oz/168g fillet of cod
or 1 small smoked trout
plus any amount green vegetables with spread from allowance
or any amount green salad with 2tbsp/30ml Yogurt Dressing (p114)

(b) Any frozen 'boil-in-the-bag fish in sauce' such as 'Cod in Parsley Sauce' plus vegetables *or* salad as above

(c) 3 grilled fish fingers plus vegetables *or* salad as above

(d) 3oz/85g calf or lamb's liver grilled without fat plus vegetables *or* salad as above

SNACK 3

1 piece of fruit chopped and mixed with 1oz/28g unsweetened breakfast cereal and milk from allowance

·Exercise·

Debbie Jenkins

GETTING FIT CAN BE FUN!

If you are reading this slumped in a chair after a tiring day the chances are you will read the headline and say: 'Oh yes? – I'm too tired already.' Perhaps you have awful memories of games or gym at school. Perhaps you have tried jogging once and it just made you feel breathless and ill. Perhaps you feel too depressed. Or, if you are heavily overweight, just too tired. And, you may wonder: 'Won't it just make me hungrier?'.

Take heart. I have seen the heaviest, the most deeply-stressed and anti-exercise guests discover at Inglewood, for the first time in their lives, that they can exercise and enjoy it. And, what is more, they feel so much better and fitter that they continue to keep up the exercise when they get home.

First, let's examine all these excuses:

'I'm too tired'

Exercise – gentle rhythmic exercise, that is – stimulates the heart and circulation and thus relieves tension so that you actually feel mentally less tired. The sensation of gentle physical tiredness you get after exercise will also help you sleep better. So tomorrow you will feel less tired.

'I hated games at school'

Not everyone likes communal games. Perhaps you were overweight then and got easily puffed or embarrassed. Today, it doesn't have to be like that. You can get fit easily in your home, at your own pace and with no one watching. But you certainly will know. You will feel your muscles tighten, you'll stand and walk better and feel stronger and more alert. Your friends will probably tell you how well you look. The most important thing is to find a form of exercise you enjoy and keep it up regularly.

Over the years I have heard so many people use exercise and diet like the stick and the carrot on the donkey, with poor old exercise as the stick. 'If I walk for 30 minutes' they say, 'I shall burn up so many calories and I can then allow myself a chocolate bar.' This is useless because the chances are you will: (a) overestimate the amount of exercise you do and the number of calories you burn up, and (b) take in more calories from that chocolate bar than were burnt up. So you end up heavier and fatter. Worst of all, it treats exercise as if it was some form of penance and food as a treat. Exercise itself can be a treat.

Think about it. Perhaps you have always enjoyed dancing or swimming. Perhaps you like going for country walks and looking for wild flowers or perhaps you have always wanted to learn to play tennis or go horse riding. Well, this is the time to start. Make the exercise itself something to look forward to. Or if you don't feel up to horse riding or windsurfing yet, use it as a goal to work towards once you are fit. And being fit itself is quite a big bonus. Feeling good is a treat in itself.

If you want to exercise at home it couldn't be simpler. The exercise course I teach at Inglewood and which is reproduced here is designed for anyone, however unfit or overweight they may be to begin with. Do this for 30 minutes and you will feel a glow that already makes you feel better. And every day you will find the exercises easier and your body fitter. So you can gradually increase the repetitions and get fitter still!

So, get started. Push back the armchair and put some lively music on. Or go out and buy a skipping rope and start skipping or run up and down the stairs or walk or cycle to work. Register at your local dance class and do a weekly class or visit your local pool. They probably open early a couple of times a week so you can fit in a swim before you set off for work. And you will feel so bright and energetic the rest of the day you will wonder why you never did it before. Or join a gym. Anything you fancy, but just get started. Soon, you'll be finding excuses to do extra exercise. You'll be trying to fit in a swim in your lunch hour or using the money you save by biking to work to buy a racing bike. You'll never know what you can do until you try. So, don't just sit there . . . get started!

'I'm too depressed'

Exercise actually lifts depression. Once you start, the tensions begin to disappear and you will actually feel better. And if you exercise regularly you can really keep those blues at bay. You'll not only feel fitter but happier.

'I'm too overweight'

No one is too overweight to start exercising. Just start gently and don't overdo it. It's obviously no good to start by trying to play a vigorous game like squash but if you follow my exercise plan you will find that you will gradually get fitter and slimmer. But you must cut down on your food intake as well.

'But exercise will make me hungrier'

No. Strangely enough, exercise will not make you hungrier. The chances are, if you are saying this, that you do not eat just because you are hungry but because you enjoy food or use it to cheer yourself up. Naturally, if you are eating very little on a regular basis and burn up a lot more calories with lots of sport then you will need to eat more. But I have a feeling I am not talking to someone preparing for a marathon or the 5,000 metres. Often, the hungry feeling is just appetite stimulated by habit or boredom and if you exercise in this condition then you will feel the 'hunger' disappear. And when you next eat you will feel like eating less. Gradually as you get to know your body you will find that you give it what it needs and *not* what you think it wants. Exercise helps you get to know your body and tune in your actual needs.

THE BENEFITS OF EXERCISE

- It improves the condition of your heart and can protect against heart disease.
- It stimulates the body's own natural maintenance. Your circulation will improve and, incidentally, you may well find that you get fewer colds and flu. Your body will actually stay younger.
- Exercise gives you stamina and strength. Your muscles will feel tighter and your posture will improve. You will also feel mentally more alert and find it easier to cope with work pressures and stress.
- Exercise can actually relieve tension, depression and stress.
- It will help you get slim and stay slim.
- Exercise can be fun!

HELPFUL HINTS

1 Wear comfortable clothes. Natural fibres are less likely to make you feel sweaty and sticky. And if you exercise outside keep warm. Keep your head warm in winter.
2 Wear the right shoes – especially for jogging.
3 Don't exercise for at least an hour after a meal. This obviously depends on the size. You shouldn't do any vigorous exercise at least 3 hours after a heavy meal.
4 Don't exercise if you feel really ill or flaked-out or if you have a bad cold.
5 If you must smoke – and it's much better if you don't – then don't smoke for an hour before or after taking exercise.
6 If you have high blood pressure, heart disease, chest trouble, or suffer from any back injury, then check with your doctor before beginning any exercise programme.
7 Nice and easy does it. Begin any type of exercise with simple warm-up exercises. Either the ones I give here or your own. But do warm up your muscles. It is cold muscles that get strained. Also don't expect to get fit overnight. You will feel the benefits of regular exercise even after a week but you can't expect to get fit that quickly especially if you've never been fit. It will take several months. Give

Mobility to music – good fun in a group exercise class

it time and you'll soon notice the benefits. If you've never jogged before, start with a regular brisk walk. Then set up a pattern of 5 minutes walking, followed by 5 repetitions of jogging for 15 seconds, followed by walking for 15 seconds. Then walk for another 5 minutes. Then, repeat the 15 seconds' jogging and 15 seconds' walking. End by walking for 5 minutes. And use the same pattern for any vigorous exercise: start gradually and build up little by little. You'll be amazed at how quickly your body responds and you will be able to do more and more.

8 Keep to your new balanced lifestyle diet. Combine the two: exercise and natural balanced way of eating. You will not only improve the shape of your body (and exercise will not make you look like an Eastern European athlete, don't forget that virtually all actors and actresses exercise regularly to keep in shape) but you will also improve your general state of health and well-being. You'll become fit and slim. You really can do it!

Now for the exercises: we start with a simple series of warm-up exercises. These should be done before any other exercise routine.

WARM-UP

For exercises, stand with your feet apart, slightly wider than hip width. Keep your stomach muscles pulled in tight and keep your back straight.

1 Shoulder Mobility
Lift alternate shoulders up towards your ear. Repeat eight times. Then rotate alternate shoulders backwards for eight counts and then forwards.

2 Arm Rotation
Raise your right arm up towards the ceiling and rotate the arm backwards, repeat with your left arm. Work on alternate arms for eight counts.

3 Neck Mobility
Keep your shoulders facing forwards, turn your head to the right and slowly turn your head to the left. Repeat for eight counts.

Now stand with legs further apart – turn your right foot and turn your body to face the wall to your right.

4 Waist Stretches
Place your hands on the outside of your thighs. Keep your body straight, lean over to the right side supporting some of your bodyweight on your right hand. Hold for 4 seconds and then change sides. Repeat through four times.

5 Hip Rotation
Hands on hips, keep your shoulders and head still and rotate your hips four times to the left and four times to the right. Repeat.

Now stand with legs further apart – turn your right foot and turn your body to face the wall to your right.

6 Groin Stretch
Bend your right knee. Make sure your right knee is above the heel. Back leg straight, foot flat on the floor. Hold for 6 seconds, then turn so that your left leg is in front. Repeat.

MUSCLE-TONING EXERCISES

1 Quadriceps/Front of Thigh and Buttocks

Stand as shown in Fig 4. Feet slightly turned outwards. Bend the knees slightly and slowly straighten. Repeat eight times. Then hold in bent position, hold arms out to side and gently raise up and down for eight counts. Straighten the legs. Repeat.

2 Leg Raises

Works muscles in hip area and side of leg. Check your body is in a straight line, hips upright. Lift top leg up just a few inches. Flex the foot, check the side of the foot is parallel to the floor. Lift a few more inches and return to starting position. Repeat up to sixteen times and rest. Change sides.

3 Buttocks and Hamstrings

Lift right leg out behind you, point the toes, keep the leg straight. Lift the leg to the horizontal position and then return back to floor. Repeat eight times, then repeat with foot flexed. Change legs. Sit back on heels and relax. Lift the foot up towards the ceiling. Move foot up and down just a few inches, repeat 8–16 times. Place elbows on floor and repeat. Change legs. Sit back on heels and relax.

4 Rovers Revenge

Works muscles around hip area and buttocks. Lift knee slowly to the side, hold, then bring knee back down. Repeat ten times each side and then five each side. Sit back on heels to rest and relax muscles.

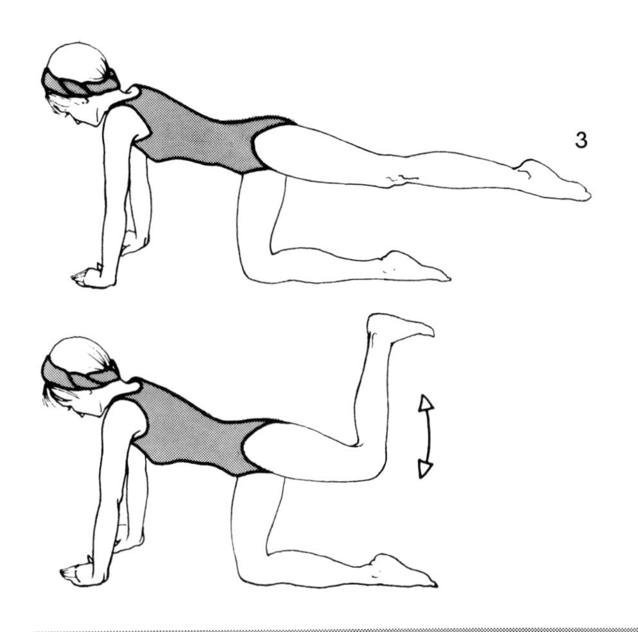

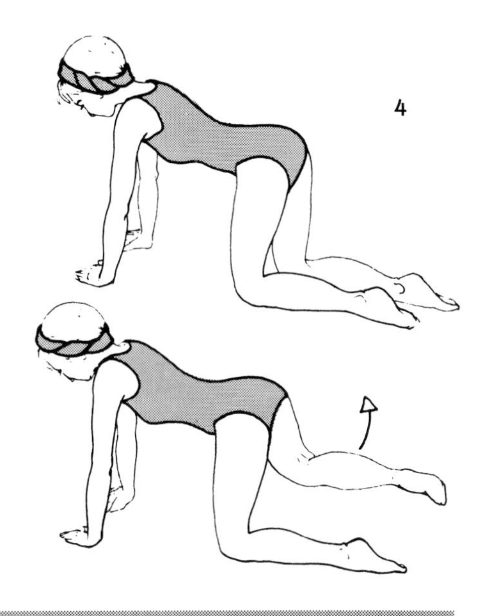

STOMACH EXERCISES

1 Pelvic Tilt

The legs must be bent. Place one hand under your back. Press the small of your back on to your hand. Pull the tummy muscles in and tilt the pelvis. Hold for 6–10 seconds then relax. Repeat.

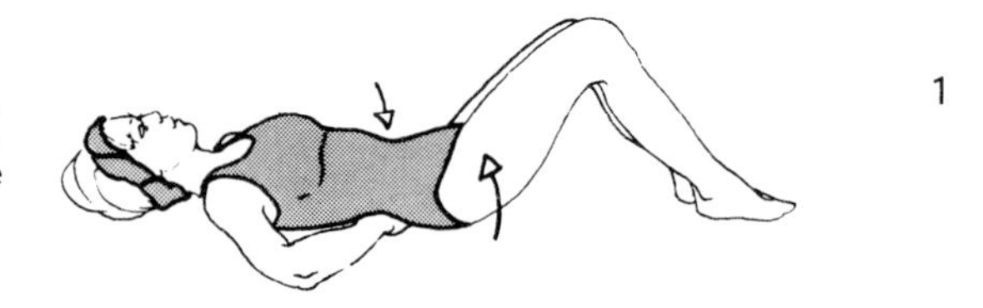

2 Half Sit-up

Legs bent, feet apart, keeping feet fairly close to the body. *Tilt the pelvis*, drop chin to chest, curl up to a half sitting position. *Hold*. Keep breathing and then relax back to the floor. When you sit up, keep the small of your back pressed to the floor. Start off with eight repetitions and then relax. As it gets easier, increase number of repetitions.

3 Waist Stretch

Stand up straight, place your right hand on your right thigh, lean over to the right supporting your bodyweight with your hand and hold for 4 seconds. Change sides and repeat exercise.

SPOT REDUCING

In addition to any other exercises you may want to work on one specific body area.

Trim that Waist

Use the waist stretch exercise above, making sure that your position is correct, shoulders straight, bottom in. Stretch gently and do not bounce.

Flatten that Tummy

Use a chair for support. Make sure your knees are above your hips. Place your hands to the side of your head. Pull your stomach in, curl your head, dropping your chin to your chest, and bring your shoulders off the floor. Repeat up to eight times, relax. As you get stronger, do a second set of six sit-ups.

STRETCHING EXERCISES

1 Hamstring Stretch
Lie on your back, knees to chest, feet off the floor. Bring one leg towards you, straight, with the foot flexed. Hold in place with hands behind the thigh. You should feel a stretch in the back of the thigh. Hold for 6–10 seconds. Change legs and repeat.

2 Calf Stretch
Use a wall for support. Take the position as shown, making sure your back foot is facing forward. (The heel should be behind the toes). Press back heel to floor and hold for 6–10 seconds. Change legs and repeat.

3 Quadricep Stretch
Bring your foot up to your buttocks, hold with your hand. Bring your knee behind. You should feel a stretch on the front of that thigh. Hold for 6–10 seconds. Change legs and repeat.

4 Tricep Stretch
Place your right hand on your left shoulder. Hold on to right elbow with left hand, pull gently, bringing your elbow behind your head. Hold for 6–10 seconds, change arms.

5 Shoulder Stretches
(a) Link hands behind body and lift. Keep your body upright.
(b) Link hands in front of your body. Lift and press your hands behind your head.
(c) Bring your right elbow towards your left shoulder, hold in place with your left hand. Repeat with opposite hand to elbow.

WALKING AND JOGGING

As with the rest of the exercises you should only work within your capabilities. You should not feel breathless, dizzy or uncomfortable when jogging. Slow down to walking if you do. Please wear good running shoes for your own protection.

Begin with walking on the spot. Make sure your heels are pressed down to the floor each time.

Arm Exercises

1 While walking, take your arms out to the side, circle them forwards for eight counts, then backwards for eight counts. (Very small circles.)
2 Keep walking on the spot and bounce arms up and down. Repeat (if you feel you can).
3 Keep walking on the spot, bring your arms in front of you and cross arms side to side. Lift your arms while doing this, above the head, and back down in front of you. Then cross your arms twice in front of you and twice behind. Repeat eight times.

Please wear jogging shoes for the next section. It is not advisable to jog with a bad back, knee, hip or cardio-respiratory problems. If so, walk on the spot. Start off jogging/walking for 3 minutes and increase up to 15 minutes. Find a nice lively piece of music that keeps you moving.

4 Jumping and twisting, feet together for eight counts, then feet apart and repeat.
5 Jog feet side to side 8 times, jog feet forwards 8 times. Jog feet side to side 8 times, jog feet backwards 8 times, jog feet side to side 8 times.
6 Star jumps. Try five first, increase to ten and so on.

Following the jogging section repeat the quadricep stretch and the calf stretch.

RECIPES

·Starters·

A starter for a healthy meal should be light and not too filling. An ideal starter is either a slice of melon or half a grapefruit. Both these fruits can be made to look more appealing on special occasions. Melon can be cut into slices and alternated with slices of fresh orange or sprinkled with fresh grated ginger. A grapefruit can be sprinkled with cinnamon and grilled for 5 minutes under a hot grill and served hot. This can be made even more delicious by pouring 1tbsp/15ml of dry sherry over the grapefruit before grilling.

The following selection of starters offers some other suggestions which can be adapted for family meals or special dinner parties.

Aubergine Purée

Serves 6 (60 calories per person)
(plus calories for the toast and raw vegetables)

2 large aubergines
1 small onion
2tbsp/30ml olive oil
1tbsp/15ml lemon juice
1 small green pepper
1tbsp/15ml chopped parsley

• Aubergine purées such as this one can be found throughout the Middle East and the Balkans. This recipe originates in Russia where it is strangely called 'Poor Man's Caviar'. In Syria the aubergine purée is mixed with yogurt and mint, in Bulgaria it is mixed with cottage cheese and garlic and it is even found as far east as India, where it is mixed with sautéed onion, crushed coriander, paprika, parsley and aniseed.

Grill the aubergines (ideally over charcoal) and turn them until the skins are black and wrinkled and the aubergines feel soft. Rub off the skins under a cold tap and put the aubergines in a bowl. Press with a fork and pour away the bitter juice that runs out. Mash the aubergines thoroughly into a paste. Finely chop the raw onion and half the green pepper and mix well with the oil and the lemon juice. Add to the purée and blend or mix well together. Serve in a small dish garnished with the remaining green pepper cut into rings, the parsley and slices of raw vegetables and fingers of toast to dip.

Avocado and Grapefruit

Serves 4 (120 calories per person)

2 large grapefruit
1 avocado
1 lettuce

• Avocado is so rich in fat that it is always a danger food to those watching their weight. Here it combines well with the non-fattening and astringent taste of grapefruit.

Peel the grapefruit, remove all pith and cut into thin slices, pouring any juice into a bowl. Peel the avocado and cut into slivers. Sprinkle with the grapefruit juice and mix with the grapefruit slices. Lay the lettuce on a serving dish, and add the salad. If extra dressing is needed sprinkle on a little lemon juice. You can serve French dressing with this for those who cannot eat their salads without it but the fresh taste of this salad is delicious as it is.

Carrot and Cheese Salad in Oranges

Serves 4 (126 calories per person)

1lb/450g new carrots
2 oranges
4oz/113g Edam or Aerobic Gouda
½tsp/2.5ml caraway seed
2tsp/10ml chopped parsley

Peel and grate the carrots. Cut the oranges in half and squeeze out the juice. Then, carefully scoop out the remaining pith, making sure you do not cut through the skin. Take off a sliver of the bottom if necessary so that the orange shells will stand up. Mix the carrot and caraway seed with half the juice. Allow to marinate for about 2 hours. Before serving, cut the cheese into small chunks, mix with the carrot and return to the orange shells. Serve in the shells, garnished with the parsley.

Celeriac and Ham Salad

Serves 4 (120 calories per person)

1 celeriac
8oz/226g lean ham
2 eggs
4tbsp/60ml natural yogurt
1tsp/5ml mild mustard

Peel the celeriac and cut into narrow slivers. Place in boiling water and allow to simmer for 2–3 minutes only. Drain and cool. Hardboil the eggs. Allow the eggs to cool, remove the whites, finely chop and add to the ham, which should also be chopped into small dice. Mash the egg yolks and gradually add the yogurt, and the mustard. Put the celeriac in a salad bowl, pour on the dressing, and sprinkle with the ham and chopped white of egg.

Crab and Mango Salad

Serves 4 (75 calories per person)

6oz/170g white crabmeat
1 large mango
juice of ½ lemon
lettuce leaves
salt
freshly ground black pepper

Fish and Smoked Salmon Mousse (page 45)

• This dish is traditionally made in Dominica in the West Indies, where both crabs and mangoes are plentiful and cheap and it is served in the shell. However, even using tinned crabmeat, it is still an unusual and delicious starter.

Flake the crabmeat and sprinkle with the lemon juice. Peel the mango and cut into thin slices. Mix with the crabmeat and serve on a bed of lettuce leaves. Season with salt and freshly ground black pepper.

Crabmeat and Celery Salad

Serves 2 (113 calories per person)

3oz/84g canned crabmeat
3oz/84g natural yogurt (preferably Greek sheep's yogurt)
1tbsp/15ml tomato ketchup
juice of ½ lemon
2 large sticks celery
2tsp/10ml chopped chives
salt and pepper

• This very quick and easy starter also makes a good snack and can be put together in a moment when someone drops in unexpectedly.

In a bowl mix together the crab, the yogurt, the lemon juice and the ketchup. Wash the celery and cut into pieces about 3in/8cm long. Divide the crab mixture between the celery pieces, sprinkle with the chives and season with salt and pepper. This can also be made with shrimps or prawns.

Crabmeat in Foil Parcels

Serves 4 (93 calories per person)

6oz/170g crabmeat, canned or fresh
8oz/226g flat mushrooms
1 aubergine
4tbsp/60ml dry sherry (fino, not a medium dry)
salt and pepper

• This recipe comes from Japan where I once spent a very happy time in Horoshima, famous for its seafood. It is an unusual combination and the aroma when you open the foil package is extremely evocative of Japan. Like so much of Japanese cooking, it uses no fat.

Clean the vegetables, removing the hard base of the aubergine and any hard stems of the mushrooms. Cut the aubergine into thin vertical slices, sprinkle with salt and allow to stand for at least 30 minutes. Drain off the bitter juices, and wipe the aubergine pieces. Finely chop the mushrooms. Take four squares of foil and on to each piece place the slices of aubergine, followed by the mushrooms and finally the crabmeat. Grind on a little pepper and sprinkle 1tbsp/15ml of sherry on to each package. Fold each package carefully so that no liquid can escape and bake in a medium oven (350°F, 180°C, Gas Mark 4) for 15 – 20 minutes. Serve in the foil packets. A dish of simple boiled rice would be a traditional accompaniment but if you want to be iconoclastic, mashed potatoes go well with it too. Real traditionalists can use sake instead of sherry.

Cracked Wheat and Tomato Salad

Serves 4 (115 calories per person)

4oz/113g cracked wheat
1 medium onion
4 tomatoes
2tbsp/30ml tomato purée
juice of 1 lemon
1tbsp/15ml chopped mint

Soak the cracked wheat in plenty of cold water for 30 minutes to allow it to swell up. Drain in a clean tea towel and squeeze out as much water as possible. Chop the onion very fine or grate it and finely chop the tomatoes. Add the lemon juice slowly to the tomato purée and the mint and pour over the cracked wheat. Mix in the tomato and onion, and serve garnished if you like, with some more fresh chopped mint or parsley.

Fish, Avocado and Watercress Mousse

Serves 6 (135 calories per person)

Poach the fish in a little water until cooked. Drain, allow to cool, remove all skin and bones and mix with the peeled avocado flesh. Blend this with the watercress or, if you do not have a blender or liquidiser, finely chop the watercress and mix well with the fish and avocado. Dissolve gelatine in a little water, allow to cool and add this to the mixture. Season with salt and plenty of freshly ground black pepper to taste. Whip the egg white until peaks form, fold into the mousse and pour into a mould. To serve, unmould and decorate with more watercress.

1lb/450g white fish
1 avocado
1 egg white
½oz/14g gelatine
2 bunches watercress
salt
freshly ground black pepper

Fish and Smoked Salmon Mousse

Serves 6 (103 calories per person)
colour photograph page 43

• This is a delicious and extremely decorative starter especially when made in a fish-shaped mould.

Poach the fish in a little water until cooked. Drain off this water and reduce in a saucepan until there remains only 2tbsp/30ml of liquid. Allow to cool, add the lemon juice and reserve.

Line the mould with the smoked salmon slices, pressing the fish into the pattern of the mould. Mix the cooked fish with the fromage frais and dissolve the gelatine in the lemon and fish juice and add this to the fish. Pour the mixture into the mould and allow to set. To serve, unmould on to a bed of lettuce. The result is a pink mousse that is white inside.

1lb/450g white fish
4oz/113g smoked salmon slices
4oz/113g fromage frais (9% fat)
½oz/14g gelatine
juice of 1 lemon
1 crisp lettuce

Greek Salad

Serves 4 (112 calories per person)
colour photograph page 47

Chop cucumber and tomatoes and put in a salad bowl with the olives. Crumble the feta cheese on top and dust this with the oregano. This salad is usually served doused with olive oil, but it is delicious without.

1 cucumber
1lb/450g tomatoes
8 black olives
6oz/170g feta cheese
½tsp/2.5ml dried oregano

Smoked Mackerel Cheese

Serves 6 (100 calories per person plus 70 per slice of toast)

• This is the easiest and quickest smoked mackerel paste in the world and much less rich than those made with butter.

Remove the skin and any large bones from the fish and using a fork, mash into small pieces. Add the other ingredients and either continue to mash with a fork or blend the mixture for a finer texture. Serve with fingers of brown toast and sticks of green pepper, carrot and cucumber.

1 × 6oz/170g smoked mackerel fillet
juice of ½ lemon
4oz/113g fromage frais

Mediterranean Tuna Salad

Serves 6 (172 calories per person; or Serves 4 as a light lunch or supper at 259 calories per person)

8oz/226g tomatoes
1lb/450g small new potatoes
1 medium green pepper
6 spring onions
1tbsp/15ml olive oil
juice of 1 lemon
salt and pepper
3 eggs (hardboiled)
1oz/28g green olives
1oz/28g black olives
1 × 7oz/198g can of tuna in brine

• This is a variant of the Provençale Salade Niçoise.

Wash the potatoes and boil until cooked. Allow to cool. Chop the tomatoes, pepper and onions finely. Put in a bowl and stir in the oil and the lemon juice and season with salt and pepper. Add the flaked tuna and potatoes and decorate with the finely chopped hardboiled egg and the olives.

Melon and Cottage Cheese Salad

Serves 4 (100 calories per person)

1 small honeydew melon
8oz/226g cottage cheese
1 orange
pinch of cinnamon
lettuce leaves

Remove the flesh from the melon and cut into small chunks. Peel the orange and cut into thin horizontal slices. Put the cottage cheese onto the lettuce leaves. Surround with the melon and sprinkle with cinnamon. Top with slices of orange and serve.

Melon Balls with Prawns

Serves 4 (150 calories per person)

1 medium melon
4oz/113g prawns
1tbsp/15ml lemon juice
1tbsp/15ml fresh chopped mint

Cut the melon in half in a zigzag pattern and remove the seeds. Cut the melon flesh out in balls and remove all final bits of melon with a spoon. Cut the bottoms of the melon cases slightly so that they will stand up. Return the melon balls to the cases with the prawns and lemon juice and decorate with the mint.

Mozzarella and Tomato Salad

Serves 4 (138 calories per person)

1lb/450g tomatoes
4oz/113g mozzarella cheese
1 small onion
1tbsp/15ml chopped fresh basil
1tbsp/15ml olive oil

• This salad needs fresh basil. It's almost worth growing a little pot of basil simply to enjoy its flavour in tomato salad as the dried herb in this case is no substitute. It would be better to use another fresh herb such as marjoram or even parsley, though the flavour will be quite different.

Cut the mozzarella into thin slices. (Incidentally, if you buy your mozzarella cheese in advance you can keep it fresh for several days by submerging it in a bowl of cold water in the fridge.) Slice the tomatoes thinly horizontally and cut the onion into thin rings. Spread the ingredients on a plate, and sprinkle with the olive oil and basil. Serve with crispbread or melba toast. The hot pitta bread served in Italian restaurants in this country contains far too many calories and this salad is not recommended as a restaurant dish because the olive oil that they use can easily push it with the bread to over 1,000 calories.

Feta cheese is one of the lowest fat cheeses and is the essential ingredient in Greek Salad; a light but satisfying lunch any time of the year *(page 45)*

MACHIAVELLI
VERNACCIA
DI SANGIMIGNANO
DENOMINAZIONE DI ORIGINE CONTROLLATA
VENDEMMIA 1986
IMBOTTIGLIATO NELLE PROPRIE CANTINE
0,750 ℓ e
ITALIA

Parsnips in English Sauce

Serves 4 (106 calories per person)

2 large parsnips
lettuce leaves

Sauce
2 boiled egg yolks
1tsp/5ml mild made-up English mustard (such as Urchfort)
juice of 1 lemon
2tsp/10ml olive oil

• An unusual starter which restores the parsnip to its rightful place as a vegetable of taste and interest and not just something to be roasted with the Sunday joint. The 'English' sauce is an adaptation of an old sauce that was used as a mayonnaise.

Peel and slice the parsnips and boil in salted water until tender. Drain and leave to cool. Pound the egg yolks and beat in the mustard. Gradually add the lemon juice and oil until you have a smooth sauce. Place the parsnips in individual dishes on lettuce leaves and pour over the sauce. Serve cold.

Peppers Stuffed with Cheese

Serves 4 (98 calories per person)

2 large green peppers
8oz/226g fromage frais (9% fat)
2oz/56g parmesan cheese
1 egg
1tbsp/15ml chopped chives

Cut peppers in half and remove seeds and pith. Mix the parmesan cheese with fromage frais and the egg and beat with a fork. Add the chives and season to taste. Take a small, non-stick baking dish and place the peppers in this. Cut a sliver off the bottom if necessary to stop them falling over. Fill with the cheese mixture and bake in a hot oven (400°F, 200°C, Gas Mark 6) for 10–15 minutes, until the peppers are tender. Serve hot sprinkled with more chopped chives.

Pineapple and Prawn Salad

Serves 4 (140 calories per person)

1 small pineapple
1 orange (peeled and sliced)
2tbsp/30ml lemon juice
1 apple (sliced)
½ cucumber (chopped)
1 green pepper (chopped)
4oz/113g peeled prawns
½tsp/2.5ml ginger (grated root if possible)

Slice the pineapple in half vertically, cutting through both the fruit and the crown of leaves. Scoop the fruit out carefully, making sure that you do not cut the skin, and cut into small cubes. Place the fruit and any juice into a bowl and mix with the peeled and sliced orange, the cucumber and pepper chopped, the sliced apple and the prawns. Mix the lemon juice with the ginger, pour over the salad and chill. Before serving, return to the pineapple shells. This is a good dinner-party dish and it looks beautiful decorated with yellow flowers such as daffodils.

Tzatziki (Yogurt Dip)

Serves 4 (66 calories per person)

1 × 15.9oz/450g carton natural yogurt
1 medium, firm cucumber
3–4 cloves garlic (crushed)
dill or mint or parsley (optional)
capers (optional)
cucumber, green pepper, carrot sticks

Peel the cucumber and grate into a bowl. Leave for 5 minutes and then drain off the excess juice. Add the yogurt, the garlic, and chosen herbs and leave to rest for at least 30 minutes, covered, in the refrigerator. The Greeks scoop this up with bread (not pitta bread as you might think from Greek restaurants), but sticks of cucumber, pepper and carrot make a light and less-fattening alternative. On the island of Serifos they add fresh dill and in the north of Greece, fresh mint or parsley. Alternatively, in Crete they occasionally use capers.

·Soups·

Soups are divided into two sections: Starter soups and whole meal soups. Occasionally one of the former such as Potato, Onion and Celery Soup will be adequate, with some fruit, for a very light lunch or supper. The whole meal soups, however, are more filling and ideal for cold winter days.

Starter·Soups

Cabbage Soup

Serves 4 (133 calories per person)

Remove the rough outer leaves and stem and finely shred the cabbage. Sweat the finely chopped onion in the oil for about 5 minutes on a low heat. Add the cabbage and cook another 3 or 4 minutes and then add the stock and the caraway seeds. Cover and simmer gently for 5 minutes. Blend or put through the rough blade of a mouli so that the cabbage is finely chopped, though not puréed. Season and serve from the casserole. Serve the yogurt and parsley in a separate dish so that people can add this to their own bowl.

- 1 medium cabbage
- 1 large onion
- 1½pt/850ml strong beef stock
- 1tbsp/15ml sunflower oil
- 1 × 5.3oz/150g carton natural yogurt
- 1tbsp/15ml chopped parsley
- 1tsp/5ml caraway seeds

Carrot and Orange Soup

Serves 2 (124 calories per person)

colour photograph page 50

Peel and cook the carrots and onion in half the chicken stock. When they are cooked but not soft, drain and blend or put through a fine strainer. Add the orange juice, the remaining chicken stock and season well to taste with salt and pepper. Return the soup to the pan and cut the orange into slices and add this to the soup. Serve hot decorated with fresh parsley or a pinch of caraway seeds.

- ½pt/300ml unsweetened orange juice
- 1lb/450g carrots
- ½ onion
- ½pt/300ml chicken stock
- 1 orange
- salt and pepper
- fresh parsley or caraway seeds to decorate

Clear Bortsch

Serves 4 (46 calories per person)

• This is a traditional Christmas Eve dish from Poland, where it is served with little mushroom-stuffed dumplings called *Uszki*. (These, however could never be described as low calorie. They also require rather more work than the average cook has time for at Christmas or any other time, in fact a day is often set aside for making the *Uszki*.) When making Bortsch it is very important to cut the vegetables into very fine strips.

Wash the beetroot and cut off the green tops just above the bulb and boil with skins on for about 30 minutes. Remove and peel off the skins and put the beets to one side, reserving the juice. Peel the mushrooms and cut very finely and put into the beet juice. Cook for about 5 minutes. Cut the beets into julienne strips and add to the stock with the low-calorie sweetener, lemon juice and salt and pepper to taste. Simmer for another 15–20 minutes. Strain and serve with 1tbsp/15ml of natural yogurt if desired dribbled across each serving bowl.

1lb/450g beetroots
1½pt/850ml beef stock
juice ½ lemon
8oz/226g flat mushrooms
low-calorie sweetener
1 × 5.3oz/150g carton natural yogurt (if desired)
salt and pepper

Cold Watercress Soup

Serves 6 (113 calories per person)
colour photograph page 55

Clean the watercress and chop roughly, keeping about 1tbsp/15ml aside for decoration. Peel the potatoes and onions and cook with the watercress until the potatoes are soft. Blend, or put through a mouli and allow to cool thoroughly. Finely chop the chives and mix these with the yogurt. Add the watercress and potato mixture a little at a time and mix well together. Season well with salt and freshly ground black pepper. Decorate with the remaining watercress leaves and chill in the refrigerator.

5 bunches watercress
12oz/340g potatoes
2 medium onions
1tbsp/15ml chives
1 × 15.9oz/450g carton natural yogurt
salt
freshly ground black pepper

Curried Parsnip Soup

Serves 4 (83 calories per person)

Peel and chop the onion and parsnip. Melt the low-fat spread in a little water and add the parsnip, onion, garlic and curry powder. Cook gently for a few minutes. Add the beef stock and cook until the parsnip is completely soft. Blend or put through a fine strainer and then return to the pan. Add the milk and taste for seasoning, adding a little more curry powder if you wish, although the flavour is meant to be subtle. Serve with a few crushed cumin seeds.

1 large parsnip
1 medium onion
1pt/600ml beef stock
1 clove garlic, crushed
1 level tsp/5ml curry powder
1oz/28g low-fat spread
½pt/300ml skimmed milk
cumin seeds to garnish

Carrot and Orange Soup – an ideal combination (page 49)

Five-minute Tomato Soup

Serves 2 (70 calories per person)

1 × 14oz/397g can chopped tomatoes
1tsp/5ml tomato purée
½ clove garlic
2tsp/10ml dried Italian herbs (such as basil or oregano)
or 1tbsp/15ml fresh herbs
2tbsp/30ml dry sherry
2tsp/10ml sunflower oil
4fl oz/113ml water (1 wineglass)

Peel the garlic, put through a garlic press and into a saucepan with the herbs and the oil. Heat through gently for one minute then add the tomato purée, the tomatoes and the water. Cook for 2 minutes then put through a fine strainer and return to the pan. Add the sherry, reheat and serve.

French Onion Soup

Serves 2 (144 calories per person)

4 onions
1 × 15oz/425g can consommé
1oz/28g Edam
1 slice (1½oz/42g) wholemeal bread

• This is a quick recipe when you want a hot, satisfying soup in a rush.

Peel and chop the onion finely and cook in the consommé until the onion is completely soft. Toast the bread and cover with grated Edam. Grill for a couple of minutes and cut into small squares. Pour the soup into two bowls and throw in the toasted cheese chunks.

Garlic Soup

Serves 4 (almost non-calorific – about 2 calories per person)

1 head garlic
2tsp/10ml paprika
bunch parsley
2pt/1.1L water

Peel the garlic into cloves but do not crush. Place in saucepan and cover with the water. Add the paprika and boil for around 1 hour until garlic is completely soft. Strain through a fine strainer into serving bowl and add the parsley, chopped, and another sprinkle of paprika. Do not be scared by the amount of garlic. The long boiling dissipates the taste and you end with an aromatic liquid which many people who have tasted it in my house cannot place. A light and certainly non-fattening way to begin a meal.

Gazpacho

Serves 4 (75 calories per person)

2lb/900g tomatoes
2 medium onions
2 green peppers
1 red pepper
2 cucumbers
2tbsp/30ml fresh basil (or parsley)
4 cloves garlic
salt and pepper
½pt/300ml water

Take a large bowl and put in the garlic, crushed, a pinch of salt and pepper and the tomatoes, peeled and roughly chopped. Slice the onions, 1 green pepper and half the red pepper, 1 cucumber and add these. Chop the basil (or parsley, although this really changes the taste) and mix in. Liquidise or blend, add the water and chill. This must be served very cold. Serve with the other cucumber, sliced, and sliced remaining peppers. Garlic croutons are also customary. Make these less fattening by rubbing bread with a little crushed garlic and toasting. Add 70 calories for each slice to overall total.

Greek Egg and Lemon Soup

Serves 2 (90 calories per person)

• Make sure that your eggs come from a source which is salmonella free.

Cook the rice in the chicken stock until it is tender. Beat the egg and add the lemon juice. Gradually pour about half the stock into the bowl containing the egg and lemon, beating as you do so, until you have a smooth liquid. Return to the pan and stir well together. Heat through but do *not* allow to boil (or you will have a scrambled egg).

1 egg
juice of 1 lemon
1oz/28g long grain rice
½pt/300ml chicken stock

Minestrone

Serves 4 (81 calories per person plus 50 calories for the parmesan)

• Every Italian cook (and every district) has her own version of this delicious, filling soup which makes an excellent lunch or supper dish. You can add any vegetable you like to the basic soup according to the season and bearing in mind the calorie differences. (See Appendix 1.)

Finely slice the onion and crush the garlic and sweat for 2 minutes in a non-stick saucepan with a little oil. Add the remaining vegetables, peeled and chopped, the stock, the tomato purée, the pasta and the herbs and simmer for 30 minutes. Season to taste and serve with, if possible, freshly grated parmesan.

Basic Soup
1 onion
2 sticks celery
1 green pepper
2 carrots
2 cloves garlic
1 × 15oz/425g can tomatoes
1oz/28g pasta
1½pt/850ml beef stock
basil, thyme, oregano
1tbsp/15ml tomato purée
2oz/56g parmesan
1tsp/5ml sunflower oil
salt and pepper

Mushroom and Tarragon Soup

Serves 4 (38 calories per person)

Finely chop the mushrooms and put in a saucepan with the stock and half the tarragon. Allow to simmer for 5 minutes, then blend or sieve. Return to the saucepan, add the milk and the remainder of the tarragon. Reheat but do not allow to boil. Serve with a little chopped fresh tarragon – if you have any – or parsley.

1lb/450g mushrooms
½pt/300ml chicken stock
1tbsp/15ml tarragon (fresh or dried)
1pt/600ml skimmed milk

Potato, Onion and Celery Soup

Serves 4 (92 calories per person)

Peel potatoes, onions and garlic. Clean celery and carrots and chop all vegetables roughly and put in large saucepan with the water or stock. Stir in tomato purée and thyme. Bring to boil and simmer on low heat for an hour. Blend or strain and heat through and serve with a sprinkle of chervil or parsley, adding salt and pepper to taste. This is a good satisfying winter soup that is ideal on its own for lunch or supper accompanied by salad or fruit.

10oz/284g potatoes
2 small onions
1 clove garlic
4 sticks celery
2tbsp/30ml tomato purée
8oz/226g carrots
½tsp/2.5ml dried thyme
1tsp/5ml chervil or parsley
2pt/1.1L water or chicken stock
salt and pepper

Apple Soup

Serves 4 (228 calories per person)

2lb/900g eating apples
1 large onion
1lb/450g potatoes
1tbsp/15ml sunflower oil
1½pt/850ml good chicken stock
pinch caraway seeds
salt and pepper

Sweat the finely chopped onion in the oil for 5 minutes until soft. Peel and chop the potatoes and apples and add these, keeping one apple aside. Heat very gently, stirring constantly, then gradually add the stock. Sieve or purée in a blender and adjust the seasoning. Dice the remaining apple, keeping its skin on, and serve the soup with the apple garnish and caraway seeds.

Brown Bean Soup

Serves 4 (240 calories per person)

10oz/284g brown beans
1 large onion
1oz/28g low-fat spread
1oz/28g wholemeal flour
pinch thyme
1tsp/5ml fresh nutmeg

Soak the beans for 2 or 3 hours. (Incidentally, many recipes will tell you to soak the beans overnight, but I think this is far too long. What I usually do, as I am invariably in a rush, is bring the beans, well covered with water, to the boil, skim, pour on more cold water, bring to the boil again and leave for an hour. The important thing is – vital if you are using kidney beans – to let the beans cook at a lively boil for at least 20 minutes.) When the beans have soaked, drain them, pour on more water and add the thyme and nutmeg. Never add salt to beans until you have finished cooking them, otherwise they turn to bullets. Allow the beans to boil fast for 20–30 minutes, then simmer on a low heat until they are soft. Sweat the chopped onion in the spread but do not allow to brown, stir in the flour and cook the roux for a few minutes. Add the bean liquid slowly until the sauce is thin enough to take the remainder of the liquid and beans. Sieve or blend and serve with another quick grate of fresh nutmeg.

Quick Bean Soup

Serves 2 (258 calories per person)

1 × 15oz/425g can kidney beans
½oz/14g butter
1 medium onion
½pt/300ml water
pinch fresh (or dry) thyme
1tsp/5ml freshly grated nutmeg
salt and pepper

Sweat the onion in butter for about 3 minutes, add the beans and water together with the thyme and nutmeg. Cook for another 3 minutes. Blend, season with salt and pepper and serve.

Cold Watercress Soup – ideal for a hot day (page 51)

Festive Chicken Soup

Serves 8 (260 calories per person)

1 × 4lb/1800g chicken
2pt/1.1L strong beef stock
1 green pepper
1 small white cabbage (about 2lb/900g)
1tsp/5ml paprika
4 sticks celery
8oz/226g flat mushrooms
8oz/226g runner beans
8oz/226g peas
1 small cauliflower

You need a really large pan for this traditional celebratory peasant *pot-au-feu*; a main dish soup if there ever was one. Joint chicken and remove skin; put into the stew pan with the beef stock and simmer for 30 minutes. Cut the pepper into rings, chop the cabbage and add this to the soup, simmering for another 2 hours. Chop the celery, beans and cauliflower and add these, cooking for another 15 minutes. Then add the peas and mushrooms and cook another 10 minutes. Remove chicken, take flesh off the bone and then return the chicken meat to the soup and serve.

Manhattan Clam Chowder

Serves 4 (182 calories per person)

2 × 7oz/198g can clams
2pt/1.1L water
2 small rashers streaky bacon
1 onion
1 leek
2 medium potatoes, sliced
4 tomatoes
2 stalks celery
1 green pepper
1 bay leaf
½tsp/2.5ml thyme
½tsp/2.5ml caraway seeds

Drain the clams, reserving the clam liquid. Cut the clams into small pieces. Cut up the bacon and cook on a gentle heat with the leek and onion, both chopped finely, until they are soft. Stir every now and then to prevent them sticking. Add the remainder of the vegetables chopped up and the bay leaf and thyme with the clam liquid and water. Cover and simmer for 30–35 minutes. Add clams and the caraway seeds and cook for another 5 minutes. Serve very hot.

·Fish·

As we learn that it is nutritionally better to eat less meat, so we return to the healthier habit of eating fish. Since, in Britain, we live on an island we have a wide choice of fish and many of them are often ignored. This selection of recipes offers a variety of ways of cooking fish and many can be adapted to include other fish than those given in the recipe.

Baked Herring with Tomatoes

Serves 4 (262 calories per person)

Ask the fishmonger to remove the herring heads and backbone and slit down the side. Open fish and sprinkle in some of the dill and the salt and pepper. Cut onions into fine slices and sweat in the butter, add the mustard, vinegar and a little low-calorie sweetener. Put herrings into baking dish, pour on the liquid and onions. Add bay leaves and cook in a medium oven (350°F, 180°C, Gas Mark 4) for 10 minutes. Add tomatoes, cut in quarters, and cook for another 30 minutes until fish are tender.

4 herrings
2 medium onions
1oz/28g butter
2tsp/10ml mild Dijon mustard
4fl oz/113ml white wine vinegar
1lb/450g tomatoes
2 bay leaves
2tsp/10ml fresh dill or parsley
low-calorie sweetener
salt and pepper

Basque Stuffed Crab

Serves 4 (138 calories per person; add 80 calories per person if using tinned crab)

Break claws, crack legs and take all meat out of the crab. Keep any juice. In saucepan heat together onion, crushed garlic, and finely chopped tomatoes, adding a drop of water if it seems to dry up. Pour in brandy and turn up heat to allow alcohol – and calories – to evaporate. Add crab meat and juice and heat through. Put back into crab shell (or into scallop shells if using tinned crab), sprinkle on breadcrumbs, dot with butter and place under medium grill for about 10 minutes until browned.

2 medium-sized crabs
1 medium onion, finely chopped
4 small tomatoes
1 clove garlic
2tbsp/30ml brandy
1oz/28g butter or margarine
1oz/28g fresh breadcrumbs

Fish in Orange Juice

Serves 4 (225 calories per person)

4 individual cod/halibut steaks
1tbsp/15ml flour
1tbsp/15ml chopped parsley
1tbsp/15ml olive oil
juice of ½ lemon
juice of 3 oranges
salt and pepper

Season the flour with salt and pepper and dust the steaks with this. Mix the parsley and oil together with the lemon juice. Spread this over the fish and place it in a heavy casserole. Pour the orange juice over the fish steaks, cover and bake for 20 minutes in a pre-heated medium oven (350°F, 180°C, Gas Mark 4) until the fish is tender.

Fish Kebabs

Serves 4 (166 calories per person if using cod)

1lb/450g cubed white fish
8oz/226g tomatoes
2 medium onions
bay leaves

Marinade
2tbsp/30ml olive oil
2tbsp/30ml wine vinegar or lemon juice

Mix the marinade ingredients together and allow the fish to marinate for 1 hour. Remove the fish but reserve the marinade and push on to skewers, alternating the fish, a slice of tomato, a slice of onion and a bay leaf. Grill, preferably on charcoal or under a very hot grill, for about 10 minutes, turning frequently and basting with the marinade. Make sure the griddle of the grill is oiled or the fish will stick.

Fish Stew

Serves 4 (216 calories per person)

1 medium onion, finely chopped
14oz/396g white fish
2 medium tomatoes, chopped *or* 1 × 14oz/396g can tomatoes
2 large cloves garlic, crushed
8oz/226g potatoes
1tsp/5ml sunflower oil

Sweat the onion in a non-stick pan brushed with a little oil until the onion is translucent. Take the fish, skinned and boned, cut into pieces and add to the pan together with the other ingredients, except the potatoes. Cook slowly for 15 minutes, then add the potatoes, cut in thin slices, and simmer until they are cooked through. This can also be cooked in a medium oven (350°F, 180°C, Gas Mark 4).

Fish Pie

Serves 4 (328 calories per person)
colour photograph opposite

1lb/450g potatoes
1lb/450g fillet of cod
½pt/300ml skimmed milk
2oz/56g low-fat spread
2 eggs
4 tomatoes
1oz/28g wholemeal flour
1oz/28g Edam

Skin and boil the potatoes until they are cooked and put to one side. Hardboil the eggs. Poach the fillet of cod in half the milk and a little water until cooked (about 15 minutes) then remove the fish, skin and put to one side. Reserve the cooking liquid. Melt half the low-fat spread in a non-stick saucepan in 1tbsp/15ml of water and slowly stir in the flour to form a roux. Add the fish stock a little at a time to form a smooth sauce. Return the fish to the sauce and mix well. Mash the potatoes with the remainder of the fat and the milk. Chop the eggs and mix with the fish. Spoon the fish mixture into a casserole and top with the mashed potatoes. Halve the tomatoes and place on top. Grate the cheese and sprinkle over the pie. (This pie can be prepared in advance to this point.) Ten minutes before serving place the pie in a hot oven (400°F, 200°C, Gas Mark 5) and heat through.

Fish Pie – a family favourite

Mackerel in White Wine

Serves 2 (320 calories per person)

2 small mackerel
For stock
1 lemon
1 medium onion
3 carrots
6fl oz/170ml dry white wine
bunch fresh thyme
bunch fresh parsley
4 whole black peppercorns
1 bay leaf
lemon slices

Get your fishmonger to clean the fish and remove their heads. Slice the lemon, carrots and onion and put together with the other stock ingredients and boil in an uncovered saucepan for 20 minutes. Put the fish into a large enough casserole so that they can lie flat and strain the stock over them. Poach on a low heat for 15–20 minutes. Remove from stock and serve garnished with lemon slices and parsley.

Malaysian Fish Curry

Serves 4 (233 calories per person)

4 × 6oz/170g cod steaks
2 medium onions
1tsp/5ml coriander seeds
1tsp/5ml cumin seeds
½tsp/2.5ml chilli powder
1tsp/5ml turmeric
1tsp/5ml grated ginger root
1tsp/5ml curry powder
1tbsp/15ml vegetable oil
¼pt/150ml skimmed milk
4 rings pineapple

If the fish is frozen, defrost in a little of the milk then drain and put to one side. Crush all the dried spices together in a pestle and mortar (or electric grinder). Finely chop the onions and sweat in the oil. Add the spices and mix well together. Add the milk gradually, stirring well. Add the fish and cook gently for about 10 minutes, stirring regularly. Serve with rings of fresh or tinned pineapple and boiled rice, allowing 1oz/28g rice per person (100 calories) and 35 calories per slice of fresh pineapple.

Piquant Fish Casserole

Serves 2 (252 calories per person)

12oz/340g filleted cod (or any white fish)
3 small onions
4 small pickled cucumbers
2tsp/10ml capers
1tbsp/30ml sunflower oil
1 bay leaf
8oz/226g skinned tomatoes
or 1 × 10oz/284g can tomatoes
1tbsp/15ml fresh dill or parsley, chopped

Heat the oil in a heavy pan and add the chopped onion, cooking on a low heat until it is translucent. Add the tomatoes, roughly chopped, and mix together. Add the fish cut into small chunks, the cucumber thinly sliced, capers and bay leaf. Cover with water and cook for 15–20 minutes until the fish is cooked. Serve with chopped fresh dill or parsley and decorate with more sliced cucumbers.

Prawns with Rice

Serves 4 (235 calories per person)

1lb/450g peeled prawns
1 medium onion
1 × 14oz/396g can peeled tomatoes
4oz/113g brown rice
1 clove garlic

Chop the onion and crush the garlic and put into a saucepan with the tomatoes. Cook gently for around 5 minutes. Add the prawns and cook for another 5 minutes. Boil the rice in a separate pan in your usual manner, drain and serve with the prawns poured over the rice.

Salmon Baked in Foil

Serves 4 (290 calories per person)

Take 4 pieces of cooking foil, each twice the size of the salmon steaks and place a steak in the middle of each. Chop the mushrooms finely and divide these equally between each steak. Add the tarragon and the lemon juice and dot with the low-fat spread. Wrap up the foil to make sealed packets and bake in a pre-heated medium oven (350°F, 180°C, Gas Mark 4) for 25–30 minutes. Serve in the packets or unwrap and serve on a warm serving dish with wedges of lemon.

4 × 5oz/141g steaks of fresh salmon
1oz/28g low-fat spread
1tsp/5ml chopped fresh tarragon or ½tsp/2.5ml dried tarragon
4oz/113g mushrooms
2tbsp/30ml lemon juice
lemon wedges to serve

Shrimp Curry with Courgettes

Serves 4 (141 calories per person; plus rice: 198 calories per person)

Peel the prawns and put aside. Take the prawn shells and boil them in the water until all the colour has gone out of the shells. Strain into a bowl, and discard the shells. Return prawn juice to the saucepan and boil on a fast heat until the juice is reduced to two cupfuls. This can be done in advance and the juice can even be stored in icecube trays in the freezer. (If you have a store of frozen prawn juice then you can use peeled prawns or shrimps for this recipe.)

Top and tail the courgettes. Clean and boil for about 5 minutes. Drain and put aside. Finely chop the onion and sweat in the oil until soft. Add the spices, stirring well. Then add the lemon juice, stirring well followed by the prawn juice. Add the prawns and pour this sauce over the courgettes in a casserole. Cook in the oven for 10 minutes on 350°F, 180°C, Gas Mark 4. Serve this with 8oz/226g boiled rice seasoned with lemon juice and sprinkled with coconut.

8oz/226g prawns in their shells
½pt/300ml water
2lb/900g courgettes
1 medium onion
1tbsp/15ml vegetable oil
1tsp/5ml turmeric
1tsp/5ml curry powder
1tbsp/15ml lemon juice
1tbsp/15ml desiccated coconut

Smoked Mackerel with Gooseberry Sauce

Serves 2 (205 calories per person)

• Gooseberry sauce is a traditional accompaniment to mackerel, but goes equally well with smoked mackerel.

Top and tail the gooseberries and cook in very little water until they are soft. Blend or put through a strainer and add a very small amount of sweetener. This sauce should be slightly bitter, not sweet. Grill the mackerel fillets under a hot grill for about 5 minutes and serve with the gooseberry sauce.

This sauce can also be eaten cold with cold smoked mackerel.

2 × 6oz/170g smoked mackerel fillets (peppered fillets of smoked mackerel go very well with this sauce)
8oz/226g gooseberries
low-calorie sweetener

Stir-fried Shrimps

Serves 4 (210 calories per person)

1lb/450g shrimps (or prawns), shelled
3tbsp/45ml dry sherry
1 egg white
1tsp/5ml salt
1tsp/5ml grated ginger root
2tbsp/30ml vegetable oil
3tbsp/45ml chopped spring onions

Take 1tbsp/15ml of the sherry, mix it with the egg white, add salt and cover the shrimps with this marinade. Leave for 10–15 minutes. Heat the oil in a wok or frying pan and when hot but not smoking, add the shrimps, stir thoroughly for 10 seconds and remove the shrimps with a slatted spoon and place on kitchen paper to absorb the oil. Add the ginger and a good pinch of salt and the onions to the pan. Fry these for 30 seconds, then put in the shrimps again, add the rest of the sherry, stir and fry for another 15 seconds and serve.

Trout in Orange Sauce

Serves 4 (230 calories per person)

4 trout
¼pt/150ml fish stock
4tbsp/60ml lemon juice
salt and pepper
few sprigs of parsley
4tbsp/60ml cornflour
4tbsp/60ml concentrated orange juice
2tbsp/30ml flaked almonds
1 orange

Put stock, lemon juice, salt and pepper and parsley in a large casserole, bring to boil and poach trout gently in oven (cover with foil) on 325°F, 170°C, Gas Mark 3 until tender (approximately 20 minutes). Lift trout on to a serving dish and keep warm. Strain cooking liquid. Measure out ⅓pt/190ml. Blend cornflour with orange juice concentrate, stir into measured liquid, bring to boil, stirring all the time. Simmer for 2 minutes, then pour over the trout. Sprinkle with flaked almonds and garnish with slices of orange.

Trout with Almonds

Serves 4 (250 calories per person)

4 medium-sized trout, cleaned
2 cloves garlic
4 sprigs rosemary
salt and pepper to taste
1tbsp/15ml oil
1 lemon, cut into wedges
2oz/56g toasted flaked almonds

Clean fish and rub with salt and pepper. In the cavity of each fish put one sprig of rosemary and half a garlic clove. Make two cuts on the skin of each fish. Coat them lightly with half the oil and put them on a pre-heated lined grill pan. Grill for about 5 minutes, then turn over, brush with the remainder of the oil and grill. Remove the garlic and rosemary and serve sprinkled with almonds and lemon wedges.

Trout with Sauerkraut

Serves 4 (212 calories per person)

4 trout (frozen are ideal)
1 × 15oz/425g can sauerkraut
2 tomatoes
1 bay leaf
1tbsp/15ml oil
4fl oz/113ml dry white wine
1tsp/5ml paprika
salt and pepper

• This recipe is excellent for farmed or frozen trout, but too overpowering if you have good fresh trout.

Allow the trout to defrost if necessary and rub them with the oil. Pour cold water on the sauerkraut to remove bitterness and press out the liquid. Take a heavy casserole and put in the sauerkraut, then the sliced tomatoes, then the fish. Add the bay leaf, salt and pepper and the wine. Sprinkle with the paprika. Cover and cook in a medium oven (350°F, 180°C, Gas Mark 4) for about 30 minutes.

Chicken Pilaff – a tasty and filling dish (page 65)

·Chicken· and·Game·

Chicken flesh has less calories than red meat and contains less cholesterol. With the skin removed it makes for sensible, healthy eating as does game and the variety of ways in which chicken and game can be cooked means that no cook need be faced with the protest, 'not chicken again!'

Chicken in Aspic with Olives and Grapes

Serves 4 (169 calories per person)

8oz/226g cooked chopped chicken
2oz/56g olives
½oz/14g gelatine
1tbsp/15ml chopped mint
1 lemon
4oz/113g black grapes
4fl oz/113ml dry white wine
1pt/600ml chicken stock with peeled rind from 1 lemon
salt and pepper
4oz/113g cottage cheese
lettuce leaves

Remove the lemon rind from the stock and season to taste. Strain a small quantity of the stock into a bowl and add the gelatine. Put the bowl into a pan of water and heat gently for about 5 minutes stirring until the gelatine has dissolved. Add the wine and the remainder of the stock to the bowl and allow to cool. When half set, add chicken, olives and de-pipped grapes and pour into a mould with a hollow centre. (You can improvise by inverting a small bowl in the middle of the mould.) Allow to set. To serve, unmould onto a bed of crisp lettuce and fill the centre with cottage cheese mixed with mint. Garnish with slices of lemon. This is a good recipe for using left-over chicken.

Chicken in Barbecue Sauce

Serves 2 (280 calories per person)

2 × 8oz/226g chicken pieces
2tbsp/30ml tomato ketchup
2tbsp/30ml tomato purée
1tsp/5ml made-up mild mustard
1tbsp/15ml soy sauce
1tbsp/15ml lemon juice
1tbsp/15ml white wine vinegar
8oz/226g mushrooms
8oz/226g tomatoes

Remove skin from chicken pieces. Mix together the ketchup, purée, mustard, vinegar, lemon juice and soy sauce and spread over the chicken pieces. Leave to marinate for 30 minutes. Take a heavy casserole and put in the chicken pieces followed by the mushrooms, chopped, and the tomatoes and the marinade. Cook in a medium oven (350°F, 180°C, Gas Mark 4), covered with foil and cook for an hour. Serve with baked jacket potatoes.

Chicken in White Wine

Serves 2 (250 calories per person)

Skin the chicken pieces and rub them with the lemon. Put in a casserole with the onion. Chop the vegetables and add these. Pour over the wine and add the herbs. Cover and cook in a medium oven (350°F, 180°C, Gas Mark 4) for 40 minutes to an hour. Remove the onion before serving. This dish goes very well with boiled noodles or new potatoes.

- 2 × 8oz/226g chicken pieces
- ½ lemon
- 1 medium onion, peeled and stuck with 2 cloves
- 3 sticks celery
- 3 leeks
- 2 carrots
- 4fl oz/113ml dry white wine
- 1tbsp/15ml mixed fresh herbs

Chicken Liver Risotto

Serves 2 (352 calories per person)

Cook rice in the stock with the onion and pepper finely chopped. Melt the low-fat spread in a non-stick pan with 1tbsp/15ml water and sauté the chicken livers, roughly chopped, for about 4 minutes, turning them so that they are all cooked on both sides. Add to the rice, season to taste and just before serving heat through thoroughly on a low heat.

- 3oz/85g brown long grain rice (weighed dry)
- 8oz/226g chicken livers
- 1 green pepper
- 1 medium onion
- 1pt/300ml chicken stock
- 1oz/28g low-fat spread

Chicken Paprika

Serves 4 (320 calories per person)

Wash, skin and joint the chicken. Chop bacon and fry with the onions in a non-stick pan. Add paprika and mix with a little water. Add chicken pieces and tomato purée and cover and cook gently, adding more water if necessary so that the chicken does not dry out. When the chicken is cooked, after around 45 minutes, remove and add yogurt. Reheat, but do not allow to boil. Serve.

- 4 × 6oz/170g chicken pieces
- 2 medium onions
- 1 rasher streaky bacon
- 1tsp/5ml paprika
- 1tsp/5ml tomato purée
- 2tbsp/30ml natural yogurt

Chicken Pilaff

Serves 4 (347 calories per person)

colour photograph page 63

Heat the oil and add the finely chopped onion. Cook gently for about 5 minutes. Add the rice and, stirring continuously, cook for another 5 minutes. Chop the green pepper and add this and the spices, stir well, then gradually add the chicken stock. Simmer for about 15 minutes until the rice is tender. Add the chicken cut into small pieces, the sweetcorn, heat through and serve.

- 6oz/170g cooked chicken
- 6oz/170g long grain rice
- 6oz/170g sweetcorn
- 1 medium onion
- 1 green pepper
- 2tbsp/30ml oil
- ½pt/300ml chicken stock
- pinch ground cardamon *or* seeds of one cardamon
- pinch ground ginger

Gingered Chicken with Chinese Salad

Serves 4 (210 calories per person)

8 × 2.5oz/40g chicken drumsticks

Marinade:
5tbsp/75ml soy sauce
2tsp/10ml honey
1tsp/5ml five spice powder
2tsp/10ml grated fresh ginger
½ lemon

Salad:
4oz/113g sweetcorn
4oz/113g pineapple
8oz/226g bamboo shoots
4oz/113g water chestnuts

Dressing:
1 lemon
½ clove garlic
2tsp/10ml grated fresh ginger
2tbsp/30ml water
pepper
small bunch watercress, to decorate

Remove skin from the chicken and place in a small flat baking dish. Mix together the marinade ingredients and pour over the chicken, coating well. Leave overnight or at least 3 hours, turning occasionally. Cook in a medium oven (350°F, 180°C, Gas Mark 4) for 35 minutes, basting with the marinade from time to time.

Dressing:

Squeeze the lemon and grate its zest, mix this with the grated ginger, the garlic put through a garlic press, the water and a grind of pepper and put in a screw-top jar. (This dressing can be made in advance and used for other salads or as a marinade for fish.)

Salad:

Mix together the sweetcorn, pineapple, bamboo shoots, and water chestnuts. (If using canned pineapple, use only that in natural juice, not syrup.)

Pour over the ginger dressing and serve with the chicken, decorated with the watercress.

Chicken with Lemon

Serves 4 (294 calories per person)

1 × 3lb/1350g chicken
5 stalks of celery
3 leeks
2 cloves garlic
2 lemons
4oz/113g long grain rice

Skin and joint the chicken into 4 pieces and put into a large soup pan with the celery and the leeks, both roughly chopped. Chop the garlic and add this and 1 lemon, cut into 4. Cover with water and poach gently for about 1 hour, frequently skimming the scum off the top. Take off the heat, remove the chicken and add the rice with the remaining lemon. Serve the rice, which will have a delicious lemony flavour, with the chicken pieces either separately or on top. (Keep any stock left over for soup.)

Chicken Saté

Serves 4 (234 calories per person)

3 × 8oz/226g chicken breasts
2 cloves garlic
4tbsp/60ml soy sauce
2oz/56g crunchy peanut butter
4fl oz/113ml skimmed milk
small pinch chilli powder

Skin and bone the chicken and cut into small cubes. Prick the chicken with a fork and put onto skewers allowing about three cubes per skewer. Make a marinade of the garlic, which should be crushed, 2tbsp/30ml of the soy sauce and 2tbsp/30ml water. Place the chicken in this for about an hour turning now and then so that all the meat is covered. Heat the peanut butter with the milk stirring in the latter gradually. Add the remaining soy sauce and the chilli powder and keep the sauce warm. Immediately before serving, grill the chicken for about 10 minutes and serve on a plate with the sauce in a separate bowl. Saté sauce can be bought ready made in good Chinese supermarkets, though it is much hotter – and more calorific – than this Indonesian recipe which I have adapted for Western tastes.

A dinner party delight – Pigeons with Grapes (page 68)

Italian Chicken with Pesto

Serves 4 (263 calories per person)

4 × 6oz/170g chicken pieces
1tbsp/15ml pesto
juice of 1 lemon
lemon wedges to serve

Clean and skin the chicken. Mix the pesto with the lemon juice. Place the chicken pieces in a flat baking dish, pour over the pesto and lemon juice and bake in a medium oven (350°F, 180°C, Gas Mark 4) for 45 minutes to an hour until the chicken is cooked. Serve with lemon wedges.

Mustard Rabbit

Serves 4 (300 calories per person)

2lb/900g rabbit pieces
4 carrots
1 medium onion
1 clove garlic
3oz/85g low-fat cheese
3tbsp/45ml Dijon mustard
large bunch parsley and thyme, finely chopped
4fl oz/113ml dry white wine
½pt/300ml chicken stock

Finely chop carrots and onion, crush the garlic and place in the bottom of a heavy casserole. Place the rabbit joints on top. Sprinkle on the thyme and a little of the parsley. Add the wine, the stock (a chicken stock cube can be used) and cover. Cook in a pre-heated medium oven (325°F, 170°C, Gas Mark 3) for around 2 hours until the rabbit is cooked. Remove meat and vegetables to a heated serving dish and return to low oven to keep warm. Take the cooking juice, skim off any fat and reduce in a pan until about 4tbsp/60ml remain. Allow these to cool and blend with the low-fat cheese and mustard. Add nearly all of the remaining parsley. Serve the rabbit sprinkled with the rest of the parsley and the sauce served separately.

Pigeons in Vine Leaves

Serves 4 (300 calories per person)

4 pigeons
1 × 14oz/396g can large vine leaves
4 rashers streaky bacon
1½pt/850ml chicken stock
8fl oz/220ml dry white wine (2 wineglasses)
salt and pepper
watercress to serve

Ask your butcher to include the giblets with the order, if possible. Wipe the pigeons inside and out and season them well with salt and pepper. Drain the vine leaves and wrap these around the birds, cover with the bacon rashers, which should have been stretched with the back of a wooden spoon, and tie the birds with string. Take a heavy casserole and boil up the stock, giblets and wine, allowing the alcohol to evaporate. Put in the pigeons and braise in a medium oven (350°F, 180°C, Gas Mark 4) for about 1½ hours. Unwrap the birds immediately before serving and serve on a bed of watercress.

This can be served either hot with a potato purée or cold in which case an excellent accompaniment would be a chicory or cucumber salad.

Pigeons with Grapes

Serves 4 (340 calories per person)
colour photograph page 67

4 pigeons (frozen can be used)
1oz/28g butter
2tbsp/30ml brandy
10oz/284g white grapes

If using frozen pigeons allow to defrost. Melt the butter in a heavy frying pan and sauté the birds, turning so that they brown on all sides. Pour over the brandy and set alight. When flames have died down, turn the birds in the liquid. Wash the grapes and remove pips but do not peel. Place half the grapes in a casserole and place the pigeons on to this bed. Add the remaining grapes. Cover and cook in a medium oven (350°F, 180°C, Gas Mark 4) for 2 hours. Serve from the casserole.

Rabbit with Prunes

Serves 4 (452 calories per person)

Put rabbit in a bowl and cover with the wine, vinegar, herbs and bay leaves. Leave to marinate for 3–4 hours. Also leave the prunes soaking in cold water. Take the rabbit and prunes and put into a heavy casserole, pour over the marinade, cover and put into a pre-heated medium oven (350°F, 180°C, Gas Mark 4) for about 1 hour. Before serving remove the rabbit and the prunes to a warm serving dish leaving the liquid in the casserole. Boil on a fast heat for 2–3 minutes to reduce the liquid by half, scraping up the meat juices, and then add the redcurrant jelly. Pour this sauce over the rabbit and serve.

2lb/900g rabbit joints
12½fl oz/350ml red wine
4fl oz/113ml wine vinegar
8oz/226g dried prunes
2tbsp/30ml redcurrant jelly
2 bay leaves
pinch of thyme, marjoram and parsley
few crushed juniper berries

Roast Spring Chicken with Cardamon Stuffing

Serves 4 (290 calories per person)

Clean the chickens thoroughly and rub them inside and out with salt. Finely chop the onions and sweat in the oil until soft. Peel the cardamons and crush the seeds with the back of a wooden spoon. Add these to the onions and stir well. Chop the chicken livers into five pieces and add these to the mixture. Cook them until they change colour. Simmer for another 7–8 minutes, then remove from the heat and add the breadcrumbs. Check the seasoning. Stuff half the mixture into each chicken. Roast the spring chickens in a hot pre-heated oven (400°F, 200°C, Gas Mark 6) for 35–40 minutes.

2 small spring chickens
2tsp/10ml salt
2 medium onions
4oz/113g chicken livers
2oz/56g fresh white breadcrumbs
3 whole cardamons
1tbsp/15ml vegetable oil

Sweet and Sour Chicken

Serves 4 (250 calories per person)

Remove skin and any fat from the chicken joints, and sauté for 3–4 minutes in the oil. Add the soy sauce, pineapple, chopped, and stock, and simmer for 25–30 minutes. Add the beansprouts, celery, mushrooms and kidney beans and cook for a further 15 minutes. Blend cornflour with a little cold water and stir into chicken mixture. Season to taste with salt and freshly ground black pepper and serve sprinkled with toasted almonds with brown rice, allowing 100 calories for each 1oz/28g (weighed dry).

4 chicken joints
1tsp/5ml oil
1tbsp/15ml soy sauce
8oz/226g beansprouts
2 sticks celery
2oz/56g mushrooms
2oz/56g pineapple, fresh or canned in natural juice
3oz/85g red kidney beans, cooked or canned
¼pt/150ml chicken stock
1tbsp/15ml cornflour
salt and freshly ground black pepper
1oz/28g flaked almonds, toasted

·Meat·

In the West we eat too much meat, although as a nation brought up on 'meat and two veg', we generally find it hard to cut out altogether. In these recipes, in many cases, the quantity of meat is smaller than you may be used to, as other ingredients such as fruit, rice and beans are included in the recipe.

Apples Stuffed with Meat

Serves 4 (185 calories per person)

4 large cooking apples
salt and pepper

Filling
1 onion
8oz/226g minced beef
½tsp/2.5ml cinnamon
½tsp/2.5ml ground cumin
2 cloves crushed garlic

Sauce
1oz/28g low-fat spread
3tbsp/45ml vinegar
6tbsp/90ml water
1tbsp/15ml liquid sweetener

Fry the mince in a non-stick pan and drain off the fat. Chop the onion and add this to the meat with the other filling ingredients. Cook on a slow heat for 5 minutes. Wash and core the apples and place in a shallow baking dish. Fill with meat mixture, dot with low-fat spread and season with salt and pepper. Pour in enough water to cover the bottom of the dish. Bake in a pre-heated moderate oven (375°F, 190°C, Gas Mark 5) until the apples are tender but not squashy (30–40 minutes). Ten minutes before the apples are done mix the sauce ingredients and pour them over the stuffed apples.

Beef and Sweetcorn Casserole

Serves 4 (229 calories per person)

12oz/340g stewing steak
1 medium onion
1 × 15oz/425g can French onion soup
1 × 14oz/397g can peeled tomatoes
½tsp/2.5ml chilli powder
½tsp/2.5ml cinnamon
1 clove garlic
1 × 7oz/198g can sweetcorn
1 × 5oz/141g can red kidney beans

• This is a very useful recipe when you don't have much time to prepare a meal.

Cube the meat and remove all visible fat and put into a heavy casserole with the onion and garlic, chopped, the onion soup and the tomatoes and spices. Cook in a medium-low oven (325°F, 170°C, Gas Mark 3) for 1½ hours. Drain the sweetcorn and beans and add to the stew. Cook for another half hour. This recipe is ideally suited to a slow cooker, in which case add all the ingredients at the beginning. Serve the stew with wholewheat noodles allowing 1oz/28g (weighed dry) per person, around 100 calories.

Chilli Con Carne

Serves 4 (415 calories per person)

• The authentic Mexican Chilli Con Carne has no tomatoes but a great deal more chilli than this version which is, in fact, Texan.

Fry the mince in a heavy non-stick casserole and drain off all the fat. Finely chop the onions and add these to the meat. If using dry beans these should be soaked and then drained and boiled for 1 hour prior to making the chilli, then drain and add to the meat. Pour in the tomatoes with the juice, add the chilli powder, the oregano and stir well. Cover the casserole with a lid and simmer on top of the stove for 1 hour. If the stew appears to dry out, add some water mixed with a beef stock cube. Taste and season with salt and pepper and serve from the casserole.

1lb/450g lean minced beef
12oz/340g dried
or 2 × 15oz/425g cans red kidney beans
2 medium onions
1 × 28oz/800g can tomatoes
1–2tsp/5–10ml chilli powder (depending on strength of powder)
½tsp/2.5ml oregano
salt and pepper

Hunter's Pie

Serves 4 (268 calories per person)

Cook the mince on a high heat, then mix in the cinnamon. Peel and slice the onions and potatoes and slice the apples and courgettes. Take a heavy casserole and cover the bottom with a layer of apples. Then sprinkle on some onions, followed by potatoes, then half the meat. Then add half the courgettes and the remainder of the onions, apples, meat and courgettes in layers, finishing up with the potatoes. Mix the tomato purée with the stock and pour over the stew. Finally, grate on the cheese and then the nutmeg, and cook in a medium oven (350°F, 180°C, Gas Mark 4) for about 1½ hours.

12oz/340g best minced beef
2 medium onions
12oz/340g potatoes
3 eating apples
6oz/170g courgettes
1tbsp/15ml tomato purée
1tsp/5ml nutmeg
½tsp/2.5ml cinnamon
1oz/28g Edam
1pt/600ml beef stock

Meatloaf with Courgettes

Serves 4 (250 calories per person)

Wash and top and tail the courgettes and grate them on the rough side of a grater. Peel and grate the onion and crumb the bread. Mix with the meat, add the other ingredients and mix well together. Place in a 2lb/900g non-stick loaf tin. Bake in a medium oven (350°F, 180°C, Gas Mark 4). Turn out and serve hot or cold.

Tomato Sauce

If serving hot, the tomato sauce is an ideal accompaniment. Mix together the tomatoes, roughly chopped, with the green pepper and medium onion. Add the crushed garlic and fresh thyme or parsley. Cook on a very slow heat for around 45 minutes and serve with or pour over the meatloaf. The sauce serves 4 people at 20 calories per person.

1lb/450g lean ground beef
1½oz/42g slice stale wholemeal bread
1 medium onion
1lb/450g courgettes
1 egg, beaten
½tsp/2.5ml dried thyme
½tsp/2.5ml dried oregano
1tbsp/15ml tomato purée

Tomato Sauce
1 × 14oz/396g can peeled tomatoes
1 green pepper, finely chopped
1 medium onion, finely chopped
2 cloves garlic
1tsp/5ml fresh thyme or parsley

Meat and Lentil Casserole

Serves 4 (300 calories per person)

12oz/340g stewing steak
4oz/113g lentils
2 medium onions
2 cloves garlic
1tbsp/15ml olive oil
2tsp/10ml freshly ground ginger
salt and pepper

Take the lentils, soak for at least 2 hours and boil them rapidly for 30 minutes. Finely chop the onions and garlic and heat gently in the oil until translucent. Cut the meat into bite-sized pieces, removing all the fat. Add the meat to the onion stirring thoroughly. Take a casserole and put in the lentils with their water and the meat, grate the ginger onto them and mix well. Cover and cook in a medium oven (350°F, 180°C, Gas Mark 4) for 1½ hours until the meat is tender. Season well with salt and pepper and serve.

Tomato Beef Stew

Serves 4 (305 calories per person)

1lb/450g stewing steak
3 large onions
1 × 14oz/396g can tomatoes
½tsp/2.5ml cinnamon
2tsp/5ml tomato purée
2tbsp/30ml olive oil
3tbsp/45ml chopped parsley
salt and pepper

Cut the steak into small cubes removing all fat. Heat the oil in a heavy frying pan and add the steak, turning quickly to brown all sides. Add the onions, finely chopped, and simmer gently for about 5 minutes until the onions begin to soften. Add the tomatoes, tomato purée and cinnamon, stir well, then cover the frying pan and cook on a gentle heat for about 1½ hours until the meat is tender. Add water if it begins to look as if it is drying out. Five minutes before the cooking is finished, add the parsley and mix well with the other ingredients. Season to taste and serve.

Albanian-marinaded Roasted Lamb

Serves 4–6 (270 calories per 5oz/140g portion)

1 small leg of lamb
1tbsp/15ml caraway seeds
2tbsp/30ml chopped parsley
3 cloves garlic

• This makes a nice change from rosemary.

Boil the caraway seeds and the parsley for 5 minutes in a small saucepan of water and pour this marinade over the lamb. Leave for 1 to 2 hours, turning the lamb so that all of it is covered. Remove the lamb, reserving the marinade, and drain the meat. Insert the cloves of garlic under the skin of the lamb, cover with foil and roast on a rack over a roasting pan to allow the fat to drain off. Cook in your usual way as rare or well done as you like it. Baste from time to time with the marinade. Serve 5oz/140g of lean meat per person.

Lamb Chops with Orange Juice

Serves 2 (250 calories per person)
colour photograph page 75

2 medium loin lamb chops about 6oz/175g each
1 × 6oz/175g large orange
2 sprigs fresh rosemary

Squeeze the juice of half the orange, then finely grate the rind from this half. Mix together the juice, rind and rosemary and marinate the chops in this mixture for 30–60 minutes. Grill the chops for 15–20 minutes and serve with the other half-orange sliced horizontally on each chop. Decorate with more rosemary.

Herby Meatballs

Serves 4 (303 calories per person)

Put the lamb through the fine blade of a mincer twice, mix the herbs and spices with the tomato ketchup and add these to the meat, kneading in well with the fingers. Add the egg and continue to knead the mixture. If you have a food processor you can simply add the egg, herbs and spices to the meat. Rinse your fingers with plenty of cold water and make the mince into small balls. Pour the oil into a non-stick pan, gently sauté the meat balls for 10 minutes until they are cooked through. Serve on a bed of shredded lettuce.

1lb/450g lean lamb
1 egg
1tbsp/15ml chopped chives
1tbsp/15ml chopped fresh mint
or 2tsp/10ml dried mint
1tbsp/15ml tomato ketchup
½tsp/2.5ml crushed coriander seeds
½tsp/2.5ml crushed cumin seeds
½tsp/2.5ml paprika
2tbsp/30ml cooking oil
lettuce leaves

Lamb and Rice with Apricots

Serves 4 (386 calories per person)

• This is an ideal recipe for using up left-over roast lamb.

Wash and boil the rice according to your own favourite recipe until it is tender. Finely chop the onion and cut the lamb into small pieces. Finely chop the dried apricots. Melt the butter in a heavy pan. Add the lamb, the onion, fruit and spices and cook gently until the onion is quite soft. Season with salt and pepper and add the rice mixing the ingredients together. Heat through and serve with the orange flower water and a few more raisins sprinkled on top.

8oz/226g long grain rice
1 medium onion
1oz/28g butter or margarine
8oz/226g cooked lamb
1tbsp/15ml raisins
2oz/56g dried apricots
½tsp/2.5ml crushed coriander seeds
½tsp/2.5ml crushed cumin seeds
½tsp/2.5ml ground cinnamon
salt and pepper
1tbsp/15ml orange flower water to serve

Minced Kebabs

Serves 4 (305 calories per person)

• These kebabs are delicious accompanied by a bowl of yogurt seasoned with salt and pepper and plenty of chopped fresh mint.

Remove all fat from meat, cut into chunks and finely mince twice or grind it in a blender until smooth. Grate the onions letting the juice fall into the meat then add these and the other ingredients keeping the flour to one side. Mix all together well. If you have a blender you can grate the onions in this and then just throw in all the other ingredients. Roll the mixture into little oblong balls in the flour. Allow these to rest in the refrigerator for at least 15 minutes, preferably several hours (this will help them keep their shape). Oil the grill so that the meatballs do not stick and put the balls on to oiled skewers and grill them for about 10 minutes, turning frequently. Serve on a bed of shredded lettuce.

1lb/450g lean beef or lamb
2 small onions
1 egg
½tsp/2.5ml cinnamon
3oz/85g wholemeal flour
1tsp/5ml ground cumin
1tbsp/15ml tomato ketchup
1tsp/5ml dry mint
or 2tbsp/30ml fresh mint
lettuce to serve

Lamb in Yogurt

Serves 4 (382 calories per person)

1 × 15oz/450g carton natural yogurt
2tsp/10ml dried pimento
4 cloves garlic
1lb/450g lean lamb (boned loin or neck)
1tbsp/15ml chopped parsley
½tsp/2.5ml chilli powder
½tsp/2.5ml ground ginger
1tsp/5ml crushed coriander seeds
½tsp/2.5ml dried basil
pinch nutmeg

Cut the lamb into small cubes removing all the fat. Crush the garlic and mix together with the yogurt, the spices and basil. Chop half the parsley and add this and let the lamb marinate in the yogurt for 4–8 hours. Take a heavy casserole, pour in the lamb and its marinade, stir in the parsley and cover. Cook in a medium oven (350°F, 180°C, Gas Mark 4) for 1½ hours.

Lamb with Pears

Serves 4 (270 calories per person)

1lb/450g lean stewing lamb, cubed
3 medium onions
¼tsp/1.25ml saffron
½tsp/2.5ml ground ginger
½tsp/2.5ml cumin
¼tsp/1.25ml paprika
1lb/450g pears

• This is a Moroccan casserole called a *tagine* (or *tajine*), so named from the conical earthenware pots in which these meat and fruit stews are cooked. The best *tagine* I ever ate was in Ouzarzarte but I have often found it flavoured with the cheaper turmeric instead of saffron. Use saffron if you can, it does taste better.

Take a large pot and put the lamb with 1 onion, chopped, and the spices and cover with water. After 30 minutes add the other 2 onions, chopped. After another 30 minutes add the pears, peeled and cored. Cook until the lamb is tender. Serve in a large serving bowl. In an informal situation, with family and friends, set a spoon as well as a knife and fork and serve in bowls. The juice is far too good to waste! You can also use prunes which are very popular in Morocco and these should be soaked overnight. This dish is also delicious made with quinces (again very popular in Morocco), apricots, or peaches. See Appendix 1 for calorie differences in the fruit and meats.

Liver Hotpot

Serves 4 (423 calories per person)

1lb/450g lamb's liver
4 rashers streaky bacon
1 large onion
1tbsp/15ml wholemeal flour
1lb/450g potatoes
1tsp/5ml sage
½pt/300ml beef stock
salt and pepper

• Bacon is full of salt as well as fat and should not be eaten too often. Nevertheless, its unique taste is essential to this traditional hotpot which you can enjoy occasionally.

Slice the liver into thin slivers. Season the flour with the sage, either powdered or crushed, and salt and pepper and coat the liver slices with this flour. Remove the rind from the bacon and chop finely. Finely chop the onion and place half of it on the bottom of a small casserole. Arrange the liver on top and cover with the bacon and remaining onion. Add the stock until it comes almost up to the top of the onion. Peel the potatoes, slice and place on the top. Cook in a pre-heated oven (350°F, 180°C, Gas Mark 4) for about 1½ hours.

Lamb Chops with Orange Juice – leave the fat on your plate along with the bone (page 72)

Liver Casserole

Serves 4 (280 calories per person)

1lb/450g lamb's liver
1 medium onion
6oz/170g carrots
4oz/113g peas
1 × 14oz/396g can tomatoes
2oz/56g dried haricot beans
¾pt/450ml vegetable stock
3tbsp/45ml tomato purée

Cook the haricot beans until they are soft but not squashy. Drain and put to one side. Peel and chop the carrots, cut the liver into bite-sized chunks and finely chop the onion. Take a heavy casserole and add all the ingredients and stir well. Season well and cook in a medium oven (350°F, 180°C, Gas Mark 4) for about 1¼ hours.

Peshawari Sautéed Liver

Serves 2 (240 calories per person)

8oz/226g lamb's liver
½tsp/2.5ml grated ginger
1 clove garlic
½tsp/2.5ml ground coriander seed
½tbsp/7.5ml wholemeal flour
2tsp/10ml cooking oil

• This particular recipe was given to me a few years ago by a native of Peshawar who said that the recipe originated from his home town, although this way of cooking liver is popular in India as well as Pakistan.

Crush the spices and mix together with the flour. Cut the liver into thin slivers and dust each side with the aromatised flour. Heat the oil in a non-stick frying pan and add the liver, cooking quickly for about 3 minutes on each side. Serve immediately.

Spicy Kebabs

Serves 4 (175 calories per person)

12oz/340g lean lamb
4 small tomatoes, halved
4oz/113g button mushrooms
1 green pepper
8 bay leaves
lettuce to serve

Marinade
1 × 5.3oz/150g carton natural yogurt
1 small onion
salt and pepper

Trim all the fat off the meat and cut into cubes. Mix all marinade ingredients together in a bowl, place the meat in the marinade and leave for at least 3 hours (overnight if possible), turning the meat from time to time. Reserve the marinade and thread the meat on to 4 long or 8 short skewers, alternating with tomatoes, mushrooms, pepper and bay leaves. Cook under a hot grill for 10–15 minutes, and baste with the marinade once or twice during cooking. Serve on a bed of shredded lettuce.

Casserole of Pork

Serves 4 (250 calories per person)

2lb/900g lean pork
2 medium onions
1lb/450g carrots
2 cloves garlic
1 bay leaf
½pt/300ml brown ale

Remove any fat or sinew and cut the meat into bite-sized pieces. Peel and slice the vegetables and put these, the meat, the garlic and bay leaf into a heavy casserole. Cover with water and bring to a fast boil and reduce the liquid by half. Skim well and add the beer. Bring to the boil and cook without a lid for 2–3 minutes to let the alcohol evaporate. Cover and simmer on a low heat for a couple of hours until the meat is tender. Serve from the casserole. Noodles are an ideal accompaniment; allow 1oz/28g (100 calories) per person.

Pork Chops with Plum Sauce

Serves 4 (260 calories per person)

Cut away most of the fat from the pork chops and grill for about 20–30 minutes turning regularly. Meanwhile remove the plum stones and cook the plums in a little water with the cinnamon and lemon rind until the plums are completely soft. Add the port or sherry, stirring well, and boil to allow the alcohol to evaporate. Add sweetener to taste and serve the pork chops on a warm dish with the sauce poured over them.

4 × 6½oz/184g pork chops
8oz/226g cooking plums
3tbsp/45ml port or sweet sherry
low-calorie sweetener
½tsp/2.5ml cinnamon
rind of ½ lemon

Roast Spare Ribs with Apples and Prunes

Serves 2 (238 calories per person)

Trim off any remaining fat from the spare ribs and place in roasting pan. Cover with the apples and the prunes. Pre-heat the oven to medium heat (350°F, 180°C, Gas Mark 4) and cook for about 1 hour. This traditional Danish dish is served with pickles, but red cabbage is a particularly successful accompaniment.

8oz/226g spare ribs of pork, well trimmed of fat
3 small eating apples, peeled and sliced
4 dried prunes, soaked and stoned

Veal and Tomato Stew

Serves 4 (215 calories per person)

Chop meat into small cubes removing any sinews and fat. Heat oil and sauté onions until they begin to brown, then add veal, turning frequently to brown all sides and seal in juices. Add remaining ingredients and simmer gently for about 1½ hours, until meat is tender.

1lb/450g pie veal
2 medium onions
1tsp/5ml paprika
½tsp/2.5ml dried marjoram (or 1tsp/5ml fresh)
1tbsp/15ml tomato purée
1pt/568ml stock (either chicken or vegetable)
1tbsp/15ml oil

Veal Chops Braised with Herbs

Serves 4 (250 calories per person)

Grill the chops under a high heat for 3–4 minutes on each side. Season with salt and pepper, place them in a heavy casserole and add the shallots and the stock and wine, boil to allow the alcohol to evaporate and then simmer on a slow flame to make sure they do not dry out. When cooked, transfer them to a warmed serving dish and keep them hot. Add the fresh herbs to the pan juices. Heat through and pour this over the chops. Serve immediately.

4 medium veal chops
3tbsp/45ml finely chopped fresh or dry herbs* (parsley, chervil, and tarragon or thyme or rosemary)
½pt/300ml chicken stock
2tbsp/30ml finely chopped shallots
4fl oz/113ml dry white wine
salt and pepper

*If you use the first three herbs you will have your chops *aux fines herbes*, but the others are also excellent.

·Pulses·and·Pasta·

colour photograph opposite

To become, and stay, healthy it is wise to increase the amount of fibre in our diet and eating pulses and pasta are two excellent ways of doing this. Beans are extremely versatile and for anyone who is slimming they have the blessing of being very filling. Anyone dieting and taking in a high proportion of fibre is less likely to feel hungry.

Beans with Aubergine and Mushrooms

Serves 4 (294 calories per person)

8oz/226g white haricot beans
1 large aubergine
8oz/226g mushrooms, chopped
1 × 14oz/396g can tomatoes
2tsp/10ml dried thyme
1 clove garlic
1lb/450g potatoes
1oz/28g low-fat spread
salt and pepper

• This is an extremely filling dish which is delicious on its own but does go particularly well with lamb.

Soak the beans overnight. Cut the aubergine in small slices and sprinkle with salt. Leave for 30 minutes then drain away the juices. Boil the beans fast for 15 minutes in fresh water. Drain and pour the beans into a casserole with the aubergines, the mushrooms, the tomatoes, thyme and the garlic which should be crushed. Cook in a medium oven (350°F, 180°C, Gas Mark 4) for 35 minutes. Season with salt and pepper and then slice the potatoes and place on top of the beans. Dot with the low-fat spread and cook for another 30 minutes until the potatoes are cooked through.

Black Beans and White Rice

Serves 4 (345 calories per person)

8oz/226g black beans
1 medium onion
1 green pepper
1 clove garlic
1tbsp/15ml cooking oil
½tsp/2.5ml dried oregano
½tsp/2.5ml ground cumin
6oz/170g long grain rice

• Black beans and white rice are a popular combination in both South America and the West Indies, where in some areas they are locally known as Moors and Christians.

Wash the beans but do not soak them. Put them in a large saucepan with plenty of cold water and boil for 2 hours making sure that they do not dry out. Drain and put to one side. Chop the onion, garlic and pepper and sweat for 5 minutes in the oil until the onion is soft. Add the beans and herbs. Stew for a couple of minutes, then add the rice with ¾pt/450ml of cold water. Cover and cook on a low heat until the rice is cooked and the water absorbed. Drain off any surplus. Serve on a large warmed serving dish.

Pulses galore – nutritious and delicious

Brown Beans (Ful Medames)

Serves 4 (428 calories per person)

1lb/450g brown beans
2 cloves garlic
2 lemons
1tbsp/15ml olive oil
4 eggs (hardboiled)
large bunch parsley
salt and pepper

• Ask any expatriate Egyptian what he or she most misses and they invariably tell you that it is *Ful Medames*, the oldest and best known of all Egyptian national dishes. Today this brown-bean dish can be bought ready prepared in some Greek stores and these also stock the dry brown beans.

Soak the beans for at least 2 hours and boil for 2–3 hours until they are tender but not soft. Drain, squeeze one of the lemons and mix the crushed garlic with the lemon juice and oil and pour this over the beans. Season with salt and pepper. Chop the hardboiled eggs and parsley very fine, sprinkle over the dish and serve with lemon wedges.

Brown Rice with Cardamons and Nuts

Serves 4 (155 calories per person)

6oz/170g brown rice (weighed dry)
2 pods cardamons
1 medium onion, chopped
20 almonds
salt and pepper

Wash the rice and put into a heavy-bottomed saucepan with 1pt/600ml water, the onion, and the cardamon seeds removed from their pods and crushed with the back of a wooden spoon. Simmer for 30 minutes until all the water is absorbed. Peel and chop the nuts and stir into the rice. Season to taste and serve.

Chick Peas with Fennel

Serves 4 (190 calories per person)

2oz/56g cracked wheat
6oz/170g cooked or tinned chick peas (cooked weight)
4 large sticks celery
8oz/226g piece of fennel
8oz/226g green beans
1pt/600ml vegetable stock
1 clove garlic
2tbsp/30ml soy sauce
2tbsp/30ml chopped fresh dill (or the feathery tops of the fennel)
2tsp/10ml fennel seeds

Chop the celery and fennel into fine cubes, chop the beans and put the garlic through a garlic press. Put these ingredients together with a little of the stock in a heavy-bottomed pan and allow to sweat for 5 minutes. Add the remaining ingredients except the dill and simmer for another 20 minutes. Serve with the chopped dill or fennel sprinkled on top.

Chick Peas with Spinach and Potatoes

Serves 4 (300 calories per person)

12oz/340g spinach
1 medium onion
8oz/226g cooked chick peas (cooked weight)
8oz/226g new potatoes
8oz/226g tomatoes
1 clove garlic
¼tsp/1.25ml chilli powder
1tbsp/15ml olive oil
salt and pepper

Wash the spinach in plenty of cold water, tear into small pieces and blanch in boiling water for 3–5 minutes. Drain and put to one side. Sweat the onion, finely chopped, in the oil with the garlic for 5 minutes until soft. Add the tomatoes and the chilli powder and simmer for another 5 minutes. Scrub the new potatoes and cook them in boiling water for 8–10 minutes. Add these, the cooked chick peas and the spinach to the tomato sauce. Heat through, stirring well, season to taste and serve.

Dahl (Indian Lentil Purée)

Serves 4 (204 calories per person)

8oz/226g lentils (weighed dry)
1tbsp/15ml sunflower oil
1 clove garlic
2tsp/10ml crushed cumin seeds
salt
freshly ground black pepper

• Dahl is perhaps the one dish that I remember most from my travels in India, and it is easily made and extremely versatile. My favourite way of eating it in India was the way that it was served at the railway stations. Here it was poured on top of a chapati which was piled on top of several others. You took the bottom chapati and used it to scoop up the dahl and gradually worked upwards until you reached the last dahl-soaked chapati. Not the most slimming way to eat this purée! It makes an ideal and slimming side dish to a curry, however, or can be served cold with a bowl of Raita (see p97) and some raw vegetables as a light meal in itself.

Soak the lentils for around 2 hours. Simmer in plenty of water on a low heat for another 2 hours until the lentils are really soft. Make sure that they do not dry out and burn while they are cooking (this happens very easily with lentils). In a small pan, heat the oil and add the garlic and cumin seeds. Cook for a couple of minutes and then pour the spices into the lentils, standing well back as they will spatter. Season to taste with salt and freshly ground black pepper. Serve hot or cold.

Fried Rice with Peas

Serves 4 (312 calories per person)

8oz/226g long grain rice
4oz/113g green peas
1 green pepper
2 rashers streaky bacon
1tbsp/15ml vegetable oil
2tbsp/30ml soy sauce
1 small onion
salt

Boil the rice until cooked but not soft and put aside. Finely chop the onion and green pepper. Remove the rind and cut the bacon into thin slivers. Cook the peas in boiling water for 2 minutes and drain. Put the bacon into a wok or frying pan and fry on a low heat for about 3 minutes. Add the oil and stir fry the onion and pepper on a high heat for a couple of minutes. Add the rice and stir for another minute, then add the peas and a pinch of salt. Heat through for a couple of minutes, stirring constantly. Serve immediately, sprinkled with the soy sauce.

Lentils and Rice

Serves 4 (264 calories per person)

4oz/113g long grain rice
4oz/113g lentils
1 medium onion
1tbsp/15ml fresh chopped mint
1tbsp/15ml olive oil
salt and pepper

Soak the lentils for 2 hours or more and boil for around 30 minutes until they are soft. Chop the onion and sweat in the oil until it is translucent. Add the lentils (stand back, they will spatter) and mix well. Season to taste with salt and pepper and add the mint. Add the rice with the equivalent weight of water, cover and simmer for 20–30 minutes until the rice is cooked. Do not allow to dry out. Serve with slices of raw onion and accompanied by a small bowl or yogurt (a bowl of Raita (see p97) is also excellent). It is also a good and filling accompaniment to grilled kebabs.

Lentils with Sultanas and Chicken

Serves 4 (306 calories per person)

8oz/226g dried lentils
8oz/226g cooked chicken without skin
1oz/28g sultanas
1tbsp/15ml sunflower oil
1 clove garlic
2tsp/10ml crushed cumin seeds
salt and pepper

Soak the lentils for around 2 hours. Simmer in plenty of water on a low heat for about 2 hours until all the water has been absorbed. Salt well. In a small pan heat the oil and add the crushed garlic and the cumin. Cook for a couple of minutes and then pour the spices onto the lentils, standing well back as they will spatter. Add the chicken and the sultanas. Season to taste. Serve hot or cold.

Spaghetti Bolognese

Serves 4 (245 calories per person)
colour photograph opposite

4oz/113g spaghetti
8oz/226g lean minced beef
1 green pepper
1 medium onion
1 × 14oz/396g can chopped tomatoes
2tbsp/30ml tomato purée
½tsp/2.5ml dried basil
½tsp/2.5ml dried oregano
salt and pepper

Cook the mince in a non-stick pan and drain away all the fat. Chop the onion and pepper finely and add to the meat. Add the tomatoes, tomato purée and herbs and cook on a low heat for about 30 minutes, stir now and then and add a little water if it begins to stick. The longer you cook this sauce the better it tastes. Cook the spaghetti in plenty of boiling water until it is *al dente*. Season to taste, and serve with the sauce piled over it.

Spaghetti with Spinach and Cheese

Serves 2 (375 calories per person)

4oz/113g wholewheat spaghetti
1 × 10oz/284g packet frozen chopped spinach
or 12oz/340g fresh spinach
4oz/113g low-fat soft cheese
1tbsp/15ml parmesan cheese

Defrost the spinach or if using fresh, wash carefully, heat without extra water until soft and chop finely. Mix the soft cheese with the chopped spinach and add the parmesan. Pour into a saucepan. Cook the spaghetti until it is *al dente*, drain and heap onto a warmed serving dish. Pour over the spinach sauce, heated through, and serve.

Spaghetti Bolognese looks sinful but pasta is permissible as long as you don't add a lot of oil or creamy sauces; let garlic, tomatoes and fresh herbs provide the flavour for a healthier dish (above)

·Vegetables·

The British cook, in other ways imaginative, seems to be lacking in thought when it comes to vegetables. So many fresh vegetables can be eaten in virtually unlimited quantities by those who are trying to get slim and stay slim, and when you are eating a lot of vegetables it is more interesting to vary the way they are cooked and experiment with different herbs and spices. Cabbage, for example, is delicious with a little added cumin seed, and caraway seeds enliven boiled as well as raw carrots. A word here should be added about the potato. After years as being regarded as the villain in any diet – people would eat quantities of salad with oily dressing but virtuously eschew the humble potato – the potato has made a come-back. A baked jacket potato is an important staple and contains many vitamins. You can serve it with a wide variety of fillings, such as some of the sandwich fillings suggested on page 28. You can eat it with Ratatouille (p86) or Dahl (p81) or served plain with a couple of spoonfuls of natural yogurt with chopped fresh herbs. It is the fat in which potatoes are cooked that is fattening and undesirable nutritionally.

Apple and Marrow Purée

Serves 4 (45 calories per person)

1 medium-sized marrow
1lb/450g peeled and sliced crisp eating apples
½tsp/2.5ml lemon rind
pinch cinnamon
salt and pepper

Peel the marrow, slice and remove all the seeds. Cook in a small quantity of boiling water for 10 minutes. Add apples, cinnamon, salt, pepper and lemon rind and cook until both apples and marrow are soft. This dish is ideal with pork but makes a low calorie and unusual accompaniment to any roast.

Artichokes with Broad Beans

Serves 2 (96 calories per person)

2 globe artichokes
8oz/226g shelled broad beans
4oz/113g spring onions, finely chopped including stem
1tbsp/15ml chopped fresh dill (or parsley or mint)
juice of 1 lemon

Wash the artichokes, removing the tough outer leaves and stem. Sprinkle the artichokes with a little lemon juice and lower into boiling salted water, which should also contain lemon juice to prevent the artichokes discolouring. Cover the pan and simmer. Add the broad beans, onions and dill after 15 minutes and continue to cook for another 30 minutes. Serve garnished with more fresh dill.

Cabbage with Chopped Gammon and Caraway

Serves 4 (134 calories per person)

• Gammon makes a cheap and delicious addition to cabbage and this makes a filling supper or lunch dish on its own, though, of course, it can be used to accompany meat. It goes particularly well with game.

Remove tough outer leaves and base of cabbage and shred remainder finely. Blanch in boiling water and allow to drain. Dice the gammon and put into a heavy casserole with the cabbage, vinegar and seasonings and a small amount of water. Crush the caraway seeds with the back of a wooden spoon before adding these. Bring to the boil, cover and allow to simmer on a low heat for 1 hour. Add the white wine and liquid sweetener equivalent to approximately 1tbsp/15ml of sugar and simmer slowly for another hour until cabbage is tender. Do not allow to dry out, adding a little more vinegar and water from time to time if necessary.

1 medium white cabbage
4oz/113g gammon, fat removed
3tbsp/45ml white wine vinegar
1tsp/5ml caraway seeds
4fl oz/113ml dry white wine
low-calorie sweetener

Cauliflower Cheese

Serves 1 (186 calories)

Cook the cauliflower until tender and remove from water, keeping a cup of the water aside. Mix the cheeses together, add the mustard and gradually add the cauliflower water. Pour the sauce over the cauliflower, grill for 5 minutes and serve.

½ small cauliflower
2oz/56g low-fat soft cheese
1oz/28g Edam cheese, grated
1tsp/5ml made-up mild mustard

Mushroom Soufflé

Serves 2 (234 calories per person)

Remove the stalks and peel the mushrooms, wash these peelings and put in a pan with enough water to cover. Bring to the boil and simmer for 15 minutes. Strain into a measuring jug and add enough water to make ¼pt/150ml liquid. Discard the boiled peelings.

Wash and finely chop the mushrooms and put to one side. Melt the low-fat spread in 1tbsp/15ml water and add the flour to make a roux. Sprinkle in the tarragon and slowly add the stock, stirring well to form a smooth sauce. Add the mushrooms to the sauce and stir well. Separate the eggs and add the yolks to the sauce. Beat the whites until peaks form, fold into the mixture and pour onto a soufflé dish. Bake in a pre-heated oven (350°F, 180°C, Gas Mark 4) for 25 minutes.

1oz/28g low-fat spread
1oz/28g wholemeal flour
3 eggs
8oz/226g mushrooms
2tsp/10ml fresh tarragon (or 1tsp/5ml dried tarragon)

Peas in 'Cream'

Serves 1 (77 calories)

4oz/113g frozen peas
2tbsp/30ml natural yogurt
½tsp/2.5ml nutmeg

• This recipe sounds very fattening, but is not because we are using yogurt instead of cream. Peas – fresh, of course, in former days – were treated with much more respect than they are today, when they are simply served with a bit of butter and a couple of mint leaves, if you are lucky. I confess that I adore peas and while they are higher in calories than most vegetables they are also more filling and higher in fibre.

Cook the peas for 5 minutes in boiling water. Drain, return the peas to the pan and add the yogurt. Re-heat slowly, taking care that they do not boil or the yogurt will curdle. Grate the nutmeg onto the peas and serve immediately. This is particularly good with lamb.

Ratatouille

Serves 4 (65 calories per person)
colour photograph opposite

1 aubergine
1 × 1lb/450g can tomatoes (or fresh tomatoes)
2 onions
1 green pepper
1 red pepper
1lb/450g courgettes
2 cloves garlic
salt

Wash, dry and slice the aubergine and courgettes. Sprinkle with salt and allow to stand for 30 minutes. Drain away the bitter liquid, wipe and place in a heavy casserole. Add the rest of the ingredients washed and chopped. If using fresh tomatoes, add a little water. Cook the ratatouille on a slow heat for about 1 hour.

This dish can be served hot or cold and can be made in advance because it tastes even better the following day. It goes with many things from filling a jacket potato to stuffing a courgette. If you are very rushed, Buitoni do a canned ratatouille for only 145 calories per can which serves two as a filling, but beware some of the delicious bought versions which are made the traditional way with oil.

Red Cabbage

Serves 4 (120 calories per person)

1 medium red cabbage (about 2lb/900g)
1 medium onion
¼pt/150ml vinegar
3 crisp eating apples
1tbsp/15ml redcurrant jelly
low-calorie sweetener

Clean cabbage, removing stem and outer leaves, and chop roughly. Put in saucepan with vinegar, sweetener equivalent to 1tbsp/15ml sugar, and a small cup of water and the onion, chopped roughly. Cook on a very low heat for around 2 hours. If it seems to be drying up, add more water. Peel and chop the apples and add to the cabbage with the redcurrant jelly and cook slowly for another 30 minutes. Taste and add more sweetener to achieve preferred sweet-sour taste. Good with all roasts especially pork and game.

Ratatouille can be a useful low-calorie dish; you can eat it hot or cold and serve it with jacket potatoes or rice but beware of restaurant versions that swim with olive oil (above)

Sauerkraut with Meat or Game

Serves 4 (184 calories per person)

2lb/900g jar sauerkraut
¼pt/150ml water
2oz/56g cooked chicken
2oz/56g cooked roast lamb
1 medium onion
1oz/28g low-fat spread
2oz/56g boiled gammon
2 medium-sized eating apples
2tbsp/30ml tomato purée
1 beef stock cube
4fl oz/113ml dry white wine
1tbsp/15ml juniper berries

• This is a Polish dish which used to be taken on family expeditions in Poland and is ideally suited to being kept and warmed up. Also a useful recipe for using up cooked meat, though for any variations in the amounts stated, check against the calorie chart in Appendix 1.

Melt the spread in a saucepan in 2tbsp/30ml water and add the finely chopped onion. Cook gently until the onion softens, then sprinkle on the stock cube and add the tomato purée and the wine. Stir well and add the water. Allow to boil so that the alcohol evaporates. Drain the sauerkraut and place a layer of this into a heavy casserole, crush half the juniper berries and add these. Cover with the meat chopped into small dice and the finely chopped apples. Cover with a little of the sauce and repeat, ending with a layer of sauerkraut and add the remainder of the juniper berries. Cover and cook in a slow oven (325°F, 170°C, Gas Mark 3) for about 2 hours.

Steamed Green Beans (Phali Dum)

Serves 4 (65 calories per person)

1lb/450g green beans (french beans are ideal)
1 medium onion
1oz/28g low-fat spread
1tsp/5ml grated fresh ginger
½tsp/2.5ml crushed cardamon seeds
¼tsp curry powder

Finely chop the onion and roughly slice the beans. Take a pan which has a firm cover and melt the low-fat spread with 3tbsp/45ml water. Add the beans, onion and spices. Stir quickly, then cover firmly. Turn off the heat and let the beans steam for 5 to 10 minutes, shaking the pan every now and then to make sure that they are all covered with the spices, but do not take off the cover until the cooking is finished. The beans and onion will still be firm (*al dente*) and unusually aromatic. This dish goes well with plain chicken as well as curries.

Stir-fried Bean Sprouts

Serves 4 (53 calories per person)

1lb/450g bean sprouts
2 spring onions
1tbsp/15ml soy sauce
1tbsp/15ml vegetable oil

Finely chop the spring onions. Heat the oil in a wok or frying pan. Add the onion, stir well then add the bean sprouts and stir fry for a couple of minutes. Sprinkle with soy sauce. Fry for a further few minutes and serve.

Swedish-style Cucumber

Serves 4 (32 calories per person)

1 large cucumber
4fl oz/113ml fennel-flavoured or tarragon-flavoured white wine vinegar
low-calorie sweetener equivalent to 1tbsp/15ml sugar
1tbsp/15ml fresh chopped dill

• This is a traditional Christmas Eve dish in Sweden which accompanies the heavy roast pork of the Christmas Eve dinner.

Wash the cucumber well and cut wafer-thin slices into a bowl. Mix the vinegar with the sweetener and the dill. Season well and pour over the cucumber. Leave for several hours, preferably overnight.

Stuffed Cucumbers

Serves 4 (158 calories per person; 316 as a main dish for 2 people)

Peel the cucumbers, removing both ends. Scoop out the central seeds and flesh, making sure that you do not cut the sides of the cucumbers. Sprinkle with salt and allow to drain upside down. Fry the mince in a non-stick pan and drain off all the fat. Finely chop the anchovy and add this and the bread to the meat. Beat the egg and add this and the nutmeg to the meat mixture. Dry the cucumbers and put them in a heavy casserole. Spoon in the filling and add the beef stock. Bake in a medium oven (350°F, 180°C, Gas Mark 4) for 30 minutes. Serve sprinkled with chopped parsley.

2 medium cucumbers
8oz/226g lean minced beef
1oz/28g slice stale wholemeal bread (soaked in water and squeezed dry)
½pt/300ml beef stock
1 anchovy fillet
1 egg
½tsp/2.5ml grated nutmeg
salt
chopped parsley to garnish

Stuffed Courgettes

Serves 4 (286 calories per person)

Remove the ends of the courgettes and boil whole for about 5 minutes, until they are tender but not soft. Drain, allow to cool and scoop the centre seeds from each half, making sure that you do not pierce the skin below. Chop the pepper and onion finely and cook in the oil for 5 minutes until soft. Add the rice and stir well. Add the cumin, season with salt and pepper and add the water. Simmer until the rice is tender but not soggy. Finely chop the dates and add these with the raisins to the rice mixture. Lay the courgette halves in a shallow casserole, fill with the rice mixture, dot with the butter and cook in a low oven (300°F, 160°C, Gas Mark 2) for 10 minutes.

8 medium courgettes
½pt/300ml water
4oz/113g long grain rice
1 medium onion
1tsp/5ml cumin seeds
1 green pepper
2oz/56g raisins
2oz/56g stoned dates
1tbsp/15ml sunflower oil
1oz/28g butter
salt and pepper

Vegetable Casserole

Serves 4 (64 calories per person)

Boil the carrots, celery and onion with 1tbsp/15ml parsley for about 45 minutes in the water. Strain and keep the stock. Wash and slice the courgettes, sprinkle with salt and drain for ½ hour. Wash all the other vegetables and slice roughly. Take a large casserole and fill with layers of vegetables: the courgettes at the bottom, then the peppers, shallots, beans, cauliflower and tomatoes with some chopped parsley on the top. Sprinkle with salt and add the stock. Cook in a medium oven (350°F, 180°C, Gas Mark 4) for about 30 minutes.

2 carrots
2pt/1.1L water
4 sticks celery
1 medium onion
8oz/226g french beans
2 green peppers
4 shallots
1 small cauliflower
4 small courgettes
1lb/450g tomatoes
½tsp/2.5ml paprika
bunch chopped parsley
salt

·Salads·

colour photograph page 95

One of the main attractions at Inglewood is the dining-room table laden with a wide variety of salads. These show how, with a little imagination, interesting salads can be concocted all year round. The image of the dieter nibbling on a lettuce leaf has long since flown away and it is not surprising when it is so much more appetising to nibble Grape and Celery Salad (p93) or Orange and Sweetcorn Salad (p96).

Beetroot Salad

Serves 4 (38 calories per person)

1lb/450g raw beetroot
2tbsp/30ml vinegar
4tbsp/60ml water
½tsp/2.5ml caraway seeds
1tsp/5ml grated horseradish

Boil the beetroot until cooked (around 45 minutes, depending on their size). Peel and cut into thin slices. Mix the other ingredients and pour over the beetroot while it is still warm. Allow to stand in a cool place or refrigerate for several hours before serving.

Blue Cheese and Pear Salad

Serves 2 (241 calories per person)

2 pears
4oz/113g Danish blue cheese
juice of ½ lemon
small bunch watercress

Peel and halve the pears, removing the core and sprinkling the flesh with the lemon juice. Crumble the cheese and pile into the halves of the pears and garnish with the watercress.

Cabbage Salad

Serves 4 (20 calories per person)

4oz/113g red cabbage
4oz/113g white cabbage
3 sticks celery
4oz/113g grated carrot
¼tsp/1.25ml cumin seeds
2tbsp/30ml lemon juice

Chop the cabbage and celery and mix with the other ingredients.

Carrot Salad

Serves 4 (46 calories per person)

Peel and grate the carrots and mix with the sultanas, parsley and chives. Grate a little of the orange rind on to the salad, then squeeze the orange and pour the juice over the salad.

12oz/340g carrots
1oz/28g sultanas
1 orange
1tbsp/15ml chopped parsley
1tbsp/15ml chopped chives

Cauliflower and Cress Salad

Serves 4 (23 calories per person)

Break the cauliflower into small florets, removing the bottom stem and outer leaves. Mix with the cress, the chopped pepper and onions and toss with French Dressing (see p114).

1 small cauliflower
1 punnet of cress
1 red pepper
4 chopped spring onions

Celery Salad

Serves 4 (45 calories per person)

Chop the ingredients and mix together with a little lemon juice.

2 apples
4 stalks celery
6oz/170g chopped white cabbage
1tbsp/15ml chopped fresh mint
10 chopped hazel nuts
1tbsp/15ml lemon juice

Chicory Salad

Serves 4 (32 calories per person)

Chop the ingredients and serve with Herby French Dressing (see p114).

1 head chicory
2 apples
4oz/113g white cabbage

Cold Roast Beef Salad

Serves 4 (250 calories per person)

Cut the beef into thin slivers and remove all fat. Place on lettuce leaves with onions and peppers cut in rings and slices of orange. Sprinkle the chopped parsley and the horseradish over the salad and dress with the orange juice.

1lb/450g rare roast beef
1 medium onion
2 oranges
1 red pepper
1 green pepper
½tsp/2.5ml grated horseradish
1tbsp/15ml fresh parsley
lettuce leaves
juice of 1 orange

Cottage Cheese Platter

Serves 1 (230 calories per person)

1 × 4oz/113g carton natural cottage cheese
1 slice fresh pineapple
small bunch watercress
5 walnut halves

Spread the watercress on a plate, spoon on the cottage cheese and add the pineapple cut into chunks. Chop the walnuts and sprinkle on top.

Courgette Salad

Serves 4 (30 calories per person)

1lb/450g courgettes
1 green pepper
1 cucumber
2tbsp/30ml chopped chives

Wash and top and tail courgettes and boil them until they are tender but not soft. Allow to cool. Chop the pepper and cucumber and add the courgettes, sliced. Toss with French Dressing (see p114), sprinkle on the chives and serve.

Crunchy Summer Salad

Serves 2 (45 calories per person)

1 young lettuce
4 spring onions
8oz/226g tomatoes
1tbsp/15ml sesame seeds
1tsp/5ml garlic salt
2tbsp/30ml lemon juice
freshly ground black pepper

Chop the onions and tomatoes and put into a salad bowl with the young lettuce leaves. Sprinkle on the salt and sesame seeds and lemon juice and add freshly ground black pepper to taste. This is an unusual and tangy salad and would go well with dishes such as Meatloaf (p71) or grilled Herby Meatballs (p73).

Cucumber and Carrot Salad

Serves 2 (40 calories per person)

½ cucumber
2 medium carrots
2tsp/10ml sesame seeds
2tsp/10ml soy sauce
1tsp/5ml runny honey
2tbsp/30ml white vinegar

Chop the cucumber and carrots. Mix together the other ingredients and pour over the vegetables.

Fennel Salad

Serves 4 (40 calories per person)

1 × 8oz/226g fennel bulb
juice of 1 lemon
8oz/226g tomatoes
½ cucumber
4 half walnuts

Trim off the top fennel stems and slice off the base. Clean well and finely chop the fennel. Sprinkle with lemon juice. Cut the tomatoes and cucumber into small pieces and mix with the fennel. Finely chop the walnuts and sprinkle on top.

Grape and Celery Salad

Serves 4 (72 calories per person)

Halve and pip the grapes, chop the celery and mushrooms and mix all the ingredients together. This salad does not need a dressing, though the Cider Vinegar Dressing (p114) can be added, if liked.

1lb/450g black grapes
8 sticks celery (a head)
4oz/113g raw mushrooms
2oz/56g bean sprouts

Grapefruit Salad

Serves 4 (29 calories per person)

Peel the grapefruit, removing all the pith, and roughly chop. Finely chop the pepper and onion and add these and the bean sprouts to the grapefruit. Serve with Herby Yogurt Dressing (p114) if desired.

2 grapefruit
2oz/56g bean sprouts
1 medium onion
1 green pepper

Green Pea Salad

Serves 2 (90 calories per person)

Mix the mint with the yogurt, season and put to one side. If using frozen peas, defrost, bring to the boil, simmer for half a minute, drain and allow to cool. When cool, mix with the chopped peppers and dressing.

8oz/226g green peas
½ red pepper
½ green pepper
2tbsp/30ml chopped fresh mint
4tbsp/60ml natural yogurt
salt and pepper

Indonesian Cooked Vegetable Salad

Serves 4 (Vegetables: 185 calories per person;
Sauce: 144 calories per person)

• This salad can be made using any cooked vegetable and is a good way of using up vegetables. The quantities and types given here are simply a guide but if you do vary your choice of vegetable don't forget to check the calorie chart in Appendix 1. Here, with its combination of potato and peanut butter, it provides a filling and nutritious meal.

The vegetables should be cooked in boiling water for only a short period until they are tender but still firm. The peas should only be blanched. Allow the vegetables to cool, crush the garlic and mix the sauce ingredients well together, adding the liquid slowly to the peanut butter and sprinkle over the salad. Season to taste with salt and pepper and chopped chives.

8oz/226g boiled new potatoes
8oz/226g cooked cauliflower
6oz/170g cooked peas
8oz/226g cooked carrots
chives
salt and pepper

Sauce
1tbsp/15ml crunchy peanut butter
1 small clove garlic
low-calorie sweetener equivalent to 1tbsp/15ml sugar
2tbsp/30ml water

Lentil Salad

Serves 4 (198 calories per person)

8oz/226g lentils (green ones are less likely to turn into a mush)
1 medium onion
2tbsp/30ml chopped fresh parsley
2tsp/10ml made-up French mustard
4fl oz/113ml orange juice
salt and freshly ground black pepper

Soak lentils for about 2 hours and then put in a saucepan with plenty of water. Boil for an hour, checking regularly that the lentils haven't dried out, add more water if necessary. Drain the lentils, allow them to cool and then add the onion, finely chopped, and the parsley. Add the orange juice slowly to the mustard (a mild tarragon mustard is ideal) and pour this on to the lentils. Season with salt and freshly ground black pepper to taste.

Lord's Salad

Serves 2 (53 calories per person)

1 cos lettuce
1 orange
1 apple
3 sticks celery
2tbsp/30ml orange juice

Wash and dry the lettuce and line a salad bowl with the leaves. Peel and chop the orange and chop the apple and celery. Sprinkle with orange juice.

Mixed Salad

Serves 8 (81 calories per person)

1 cucumber
6 tomatoes
2 medium onions
1 medium avocado
4oz/113g sliced raw mushrooms
8 sticks celery
1 green pepper
1 red pepper
1tsp/5ml lemon juice

Chop the onions, celery and peppers and slice the cucumber, tomatoes, avocado and mushrooms. Mix together. Sprinkle with a little lemon juice to stop the avocado turning brown and serve with French Dressing (p114) in a separate bowl.

Mozzarella, Watercress and Orange Salad

Serves 4 (162 calories per person)

6oz/170g Mozzarella cheese
2 bunches watercress
2 large oranges

Salads served with a low-calorie dressing should be part of your diet every day; whatever the season, there is always a delicious combination, but use avocado pears sparingly – they are rich in fat and calories

• I discovered this combination when the avocados I had bought as a starter were found to be bad and this was all I had in the house. It is a delicious and unusual salad which can be a starter or a light lunch.

Cut the cheese into slivers. Peel and pith the orange and cut into chunks and mix with the chopped watercress. Lay the cheese on top and serve with Orange and Mustard Dressing (p114).

Mushroom, Watercress and Orange Salad

Serves 2 (40 calories per person)

4oz/113g mushrooms
1 bunch watercress
1 orange
2tbsp/30ml orange juice

Clean and finely slice the mushrooms, roughly tear the watercress and peel the orange and cut into thin slices. Mix together and sprinkle with the orange juice. This is a very refreshing salad, excellent with game.

Orange and Sweetcorn Salad

Serves 2 (154 calories per person)

4oz/113g white cabbage
2 oranges
4oz/113g chopped raw fennel
2tbsp/30ml sweetcorn
½tsp/2.5ml cumin seed

Finely chop the cabbage, peel the oranges and cut horizontally into thin slices. Mix all the ingredients together and allow to rest for 30 minutes before serving.

Pasta and Pepper Salad

Serves 2 (102 calories per person)

4oz/113g wholewheat pasta shells
2 sticks celery
½ small green pepper
½ small red pepper
2 spring onions

Boil the pasta until it is *al dente*. Drain and allow to cool. Chop the other ingredients and add the cooked pasta. Serve with Orange and Mustard Dressing (p114).

Pasta, Ham and Pineapple Salad

Serves 2 (288 calories per person)

1 × 8oz/226g can of pineapple in natural juice
or 8oz/226g fresh pineapple and 4tbsp/60ml pineapple juice
4oz/113g ham
2oz/56g wholewheat pasta shells
½ red pepper
4oz/113g peas, frozen
½tsp/2.5ml mild mustard

Place the pasta into boiling water and cook until *al dente*. Drain the pineapple if canned and reserve the juice. Defrost the peas thoroughly. Chop the pepper, ham and pineapple and mix with the cooled pasta and peas. Gradually add the juice to the mustard and pour this over the salad.

Pasta, Pea and Peperami Salad

Serves 2 (38 calories per person)

4oz/113g wholewheat pasta shells
4oz/113g peas
1 × Mattessons Peperami stick
1 × 5.3oz/150g carton natural yogurt
1tbsp/15ml fresh chopped mint or parsley
salt and freshly ground black pepper

• This is a very quick but filling salad, a meal in itself.

Place the pasta in boiling water and cook until it is *al dente*. Add the peas, return the water to the boil, drain and allow both to cool. Chop the Peperami stick and mix the mint and yogurt together. When the pasta is cool, add the Peperami and yogurt and season well with salt and plenty of freshly ground black pepper.

Potato Salad

Serves 2 (125 calories per person)

Wash, peel and cook the potatoes until they are cooked but not soggy. Drain and allow to cool. Mix the fresh mint, chopped, with the yogurt and lemon juice, salt to taste and add plenty of freshly ground black pepper. Add the potatoes to the dressing and allow to rest for 30 minutes before serving.

6oz/170g potatoes
1tsp/5ml fresh mint
1 × 5.3oz/150g carton natural yogurt
1tbsp/15ml lemon juice
salt and freshly ground black pepper

Raita (Cucumber with yogurt)

Serves 4 (65 calories per person)

Peel the cucumber and grate the flesh into a bowl. Sprinkle with a little salt and leave for about 30 minutes. Drain off the liquid and mix the cucumber flesh with the yogurt. Add the herbs, finely chopped, and leave to chill in the refrigerator. If you wish, you can decorate the bowl for serving with a pattern made from sprinkling red paprika.

1 medium, firm cucumber
1 × 15.9oz/450g carton natural yogurt
2tbsp/30ml fresh mint or coriander
salt
red paprika to decorate (optional)

Red Bean Salad

Serves 4 (100 calories per person)

Drain the beans and finely chop the onion. Mix with the parsley and serve with Orange and Mustard Dressing (p114).

15oz/425g cooked or canned kidney beans
1 medium onion
2tbsp/30ml chopped parsley

Salad Elona

Serves 4 (23 calories per person)

Wash and hull the strawberries and allow to dry. Peel the cucumber and cut into wafer-thin slices. Cut the strawberries vertically into thin slices and spread the cucumbers and strawberries on a plate in overlapping circles, making a serpent of the strawberries. Sprinkle with lemon juice. Several plates of this salad make a very decorative and low-calorie addition to a summer buffet.

1 cucumber
8oz/226g strawberries
juice of 1 lemon

Seafood Salad with Yogurt Dressing

Serves 4 (180 calories per person)

Poach the cod in a little salted water and remove any skin and bones. Sprinkle with a little lemon juice and leave to cool. Place the prawns and crab meat on the lettuce leaves. Cut the smoked salmon into tiny pieces and arrange these on top. Cut the cucumber into thin slices and place these around the edge of the serving dish with the cod on top. Sprinkle on the dill and lemon juice. Serve with Yogurt Dressing (p114) in a separate bowl.

1 × 6oz/170g can crab meat
8oz/226g shelled prawns, cooked
4oz/113g smoked salmon
6oz/170g cod fillet
juice of 1 lemon
lettuce leaves
1 cucumber
1tbsp/15ml chopped fresh dill or fennel

Sweetcorn Salad

Serves 4 (72 calories per person)

10oz/284g sweetcorn
1 green pepper
1 red pepper
1 medium onion
½ cucumber

Drain the sweetcorn, finely chop the onion and cucumber and cut the peppers into rings. Mix together and serve. Because of the sweetness of the sweetcorn, this salad does not need a dressing.

Spinach and Bacon Salad

Serves 4 (106 calories per person)

1lb/450g young spinach
3 rashers streaky bacon
2tbsp/30ml white wine vinegar
1tsp/5ml mild made-up mustard
2tbsp/30ml olive oil

Grill or fry the bacon until it is crisp and drain off the fat with kitchen towels, allow to cool and then crumble. Wash spinach in plenty of cold water, dry and tear into small pieces. Mix together the mustard, oil and vinegar. Immediately before serving, mix the dressing and bacon together and pour over the spinach.

Tabbouleh (Cracked wheat)

Serves 4 (170 calories per person)

4oz/113g cracked wheat
1 medium onion
2tbsp/30ml chopped parsley
3tbsp/45ml chopped mint
juice of 1 lemon
2tbsp/30ml olive oil
salt and pepper
lettuce leaves
green pepper, cucumber, parsley and mint to decorate

• I cannot imagine a Lebanese meal that does not include Tabbouleh. This light, lemon-flavoured salad which is usually decorated beautifully with ribbons of peppers, cucumbers and black olives, is invariably one of the many starters which begin a Lebanese meal. You can buy cracked wheat in most health shops today and it is an excellent high-fibre ingredient.

Soak the cracked wheat in plenty of cold water. It will swell up considerably in 20–30 minutes. Drain it into a clean tea towel and squeeze out as much water as possible. Put the cracked wheat into a bowl and grate the onion over it so that the juice drops into the bowl. Add the herbs and the remaining ingredients. Season and stir well. Serve on lettuce leaves on individual plates decorated with slices of green pepper and cucumber and a few extra sprigs of parsley and mint. You can also mix in a finely chopped tomato if you like to give it more colour.

Three Bean Salad

Serves 4 (130 calories per person)

7oz/198g cooked *or* canned kidney beans
3oz/85g dried black beans
1lb/450g french beans

Soak and boil the black beans until they are tender but not soft. Remember not to add salt to the water when cooking beans or you will end up with little bullets. Defrost the french beans (if frozen), bring to the boil and cook for 2 minutes. Mix the beans together and serve with Orange and Mustard Dressing (p114).

Tuna Salad

Serves 2 (240 calories per person)

Drain the tuna and the kidney beans. Simmer the french beans for 3–4 minutes, drain and allow to cool. Finely chop the onion. Mix the tomato purée and lemon juice together. Put all the ingredients in a salad bowl and add the dressing.

1 × 7oz/198g can of tuna in brine
6oz/170g canned *or* cooked red kidney beans
8oz/226g french beans
1 small onion
4tbsp/60ml lemon juice
1tbsp/15ml tomato purée

Vegetarian Salad

Serves 4 (160 calories per person)

Chop the carrots, onion and apples, drain the kidney beans and mix with the other ingredients. This salad is such an interesting mixture of tastes that it does not need a dressing.

1lb/450g carrots
1 medium onion
1 bunch watercress
2 eating apples
2oz/56g chopped hazelnuts
2oz/56g dried stoned dates
4oz/113g cooked *or* canned kidney beans

Waldorf-style Salad

Serves 4 (182 calories per person)

Separate the egg, finely chop the white and mash the yolk with a fork. Mix the yolk with 2tbsp/30ml of the lemon juice until it forms a smooth paste, then gradually add the yogurt. Season well with salt and pepper. Wash and core the apples and cut three of them into small cubes. Put immediately into the yogurt dressing. Finely chop the celery and walnuts, add to the apple and mix thoroughly. Core and thinly slice the remaining apple and sprinkle with the remaining lemon juice. Line a salad bowl with the lettuce leaves, spoon in the yogurt-dressed salad, and top with a circle of the apple slices.

4 crisp eating apples
8 sticks celery (½ head)
2oz/56g shelled walnuts
1 egg, hardboiled
2 × 5.3oz/150g cartons natural yogurt
1 lettuce
3tbsp/45ml lemon juice
salt and pepper

Winter Salad

Serves 4 (166 calories per person)

Peel and boil the potatoes, drain and allow to cool, and hardboil the egg. Break the cauliflower into small florets. Grate the carrots. Chop the egg and potato and mix the ingredients with the yogurt and caraway seeds. Season well with salt and freshly ground black pepper.

4oz/113g cauliflower
4 medium carrots
2tbsp/30ml grated celeriac
2tbsp/30ml grated turnip
8oz/226g potatoes
1 egg
1 × 5.3oz/150g carton natural yogurt
1tsp/5ml caraway seeds
salt and freshly ground black pepper

·Eggs·

colour photograph page 102

For creating an instant delicious meal there is no food more versatile than the egg. Whilst egg yolks must be eaten in moderation – not more than three a week is suggested for those who are watching their cholesterol intake – the egg white can be used in unlimited quantities to make creamy mousses and fluffy sweets. These few egg recipes offer you a different way of looking at omelettes and a low-calorie method of cooking the delicious and versatile soufflé.

Baked Eggs with Tomatoes and Peppers

Serves 4 (176 calories per person)

4 green peppers
8 small tomatoes
4 eggs
2tbsp/30ml oil
salt and pepper

• This is an adaption of the Tunisian dish *Shakshouka.*

Plunge the tomatoes into boiling water and peel them. Wash, seed and slice the peppers thinly. Heat oil and stew the peppers until tender, then add the tomatoes with some salt and pepper. Cook for 5–10 minutes, stirring gently. Divide the vegetables between four individual ovenproof dishes (ramekins are ideal). Break an egg into each dish and bake in a medium oven (350°F, 180°C, Gas Mark 4) for 8–10 minutes until they are set. Serve immediately.

Baked Green Omelette

Serves 4 (187 calories per person)

2 leeks
4oz/113g spinach
6 spring onions
8 eggs
2–3tbsp/30–45ml parsley
fresh herbs: chives, dill, basil, tarragon
salt and pepper

• This is a traditional Persian New Year's Day dish but it is particularly good in spring when the first spring spinach comes into the shops.

Wash the vegetables and herbs carefully, dry and chop them. Beat eggs and add the other ingredients and a pinch of salt and pepper. Pour into a greased flat baking dish and bake in a low oven (325°F, 170°C, Gas Mark 3) for 45 minutes. Raise temperature for last 5 minutes to (375°F, 190°C, Gas Mark 5) to make the top crusty.

Cheese Soufflé

Serves 2 (371 calories per person)

Melt the low-fat spread in 1tbsp/15ml water and add the flour to make a roux. Add ¼pt/150ml cold water gradually to form a thick, smooth sauce. Separate the eggs and add the yolks to the sauce. Grate in the cheese and add the mustard. Beat the egg whites until peaks form and fold into cheese mixture. Pour into a soufflé dish and bake in a pre-heated medium oven (350°F, 180°C, Gas Mark 4) for 25 minutes.

1oz/28g low-fat spread
1oz/28g wholemeal flour
3 eggs
1oz/28g feta cheese
1oz/28g Aerobic Gouda or Edam
1tsp/5ml made-up mild mustard

Cowboy's Eggs

Serves 4 (220 calories per person)

• This dish is not from Texas cowboys but originates in Argentina; how 'macho' the cowboy was presumably depended on the amount of chilli that he included.

Chop the onion and heat gently in the oil until soft. Add finely chopped, seeded peppers, the tomatoes peeled and roughly chopped, seasonings and salt and pepper. Simmer for around 10 minutes until the sauce is thick. Poach the eggs, remove from the water with a perforated spoon, place on a serving dish and cover with the sauce. Use hot peppers or the mild green ones and vary the amount of chilli powder to suit your personal taste.

8 eggs
1tbsp/15ml cooking oil
2 cloves garlic
1 medium onion
2tsp/10ml chilli powder
2 small hot green peppers
or 1 large green pepper
1lb/450g tomatoes
¼tsp/1.25ml dried oregano
salt and pepper

Herb Soufflé

Serves 2 (230 calories per person)

Melt the low-fat spread in 1tbsp/15ml water and add the flour to make a roux. Sprinkle in the herbs and gradually add the stock to form a thick, smooth sauce, stirring well. Separate the eggs and add the yolks to the sauce. Beat the whites until peaks form, fold into herb mixture and pour into a soufflé dish and bake in a pre-heated oven (350°F, 180°C, Gas Mark 4) for 25 minutes.

1oz/28g low-fat spread
1oz/28g wholemeal flour
3 eggs
¼pt/150ml chicken stock
1tsp/5ml mixed fresh herbs
1tsp/5ml chopped chives
1tsp/5ml chopped parsley

Mint and Parsley Omelettes

Serves 4 (153 calories per person)

Chop the onions and herbs finely, beat the eggs and add the herbs and onions, season with salt and pepper. Heat the oil in a frying pan until very hot but not smoking and drop in the mixture. Cook on a strong heat and serve immediately. If you have a small omelette pan only make individual omelettes.

6 eggs
2tbsp/30ml chopped mint
2tbsp/30ml chopped parsley
4 spring onions
1tbsp/15ml oil
salt and pepper

·Sweets·

So many sweets contain sugar that ideally, for good health, the perfect end to a meal is fresh fruit. Nonetheless, the pudding tradition is strong in Britain, and many people feel that a meal is not complete without some made-up sweet. A sweet should be light and delicate in summer and warming and tasty in winter, or at the end of a cold meal. The following selection is primarily fruit based with one or two additions for those special dinner parties.

Sugar You may note that many of the recipes include a low-calorie sweetener instead of sugar. This can be used and does not, of course, contain the calories of sugar but use it sparingly, only when the flavour is otherwise really tart. It is much better to try and wean yourself away from having a sweet tooth and eat fruits and sweets without any sugar.

Ambrosia

Serves 4 (218 calories per person)

1 × 2lb/900g pineapple
3 oranges
2 bananas
4 fresh dates
2tbsp/30ml desiccated coconut

• This glorious sweet is best known in Martinique and is reputed to have been invented by the Empress Josephine.

Slice the pineapple vertically including the crown of leaves two-thirds of the way across the fruit. Scoop the fruit out of both the deep and shallow sections and put in a bowl together with any juice and cut the pineapple into small pieces. Peel the oranges and cut them into slices and slice the bananas adding these to the pineapple. Chill. Before serving pour the fruit into the deep hollowed pineapple shell and sprinkle with coconut and the sliced fresh dates.

Eggs – in moderation – provide protein without too many fats

Apple Soufflé

Serves 4 (192 calories per person)

3 medium-sized eating apples
liquid sweetener
2tbsp/30ml cornflour
3 egg yolks
5 egg whites
½tsp/2.5ml cinnamon
grated rind 1 lemon

Peel and halve the apples, removing the cores, half cover with water and cook gently in a pan for about 3–5 minutes. Remove the apples and put to one side. Boil the apple liquid until there is about ⅓pt/190ml and sweeten with a little liquid sweetener if the apples are rather sour. Mix the cornflour with an equal amount of cold water until it forms a smooth paste, gradually add this to the apple water and heat, stirring all the while until it thickens. Remove from the heat. Whip the egg yolks with the lemon and cinnamon and add these to the sauce. Beat the egg whites until they peak and add a little sweetener. Fold the egg whites into the apple mixture. Place in a hot oven (375°F, 190°C, Gas Mark 5) for 30 minutes.

Baked Apples with Dates

Serves 2 (170 calories per person)

2 cooking apples
2oz/56g stones dates
½oz/14g low-fat spread

Core the apples and put in a small baking dish. Stuff with the dates, dot with the low-fat spread and bake 30–45 minutes (350°F, 180°C, Gas Mark 4).

Banana Cheese

Serves 2 (80 calories per person)

1 small banana
2oz/56g low-fat soft cheese
3tbsp/45ml natural yogurt
½tsp/2.5ml cinnamon

Mash the banana and blend thoroughly with the cheese and yogurt. Sprinkle with cinnamon and serve immediately.

Banana Flambé

Serves 4 (120 calories per person)

4 large bananas
1oz/28g brown sugar
juice of 2 limes (or ½ lemon)
2fl oz/56ml brandy (½ wineglass)
½tsp/2.5ml cinnamon

Peel the bananas. Cut in half lengthwise and place in a shallow fireproof dish. Sprinkle with the sugar, cinnamon and lime juice – and do try to find fresh limes, the taste is so much better than lemon – and 2tbsp/30ml of the brandy. Grill under a medium hot grill for about 10 minutes, turning the bananas regularly. Before serving gently heat the remainder of the brandy, pour over the bananas and set alight.

Blackberry Sorbet

Serves 4 (40 calories per person)

1lb/450g blackberries
2 egg whites
low-calorie sweetener

• This can be made equally well with strawberries, raspberries or blackcurrants. Adjust the sweetening in each case and the calories according to the guide in Appendix 1.

Mash or liquidise the blackberries and put through a strainer. Sweeten to taste but do not over-sweeten as a sorbet should be refreshingly tangy. Whip the egg whites until peaks form and add to the blackberries. Put into a metal or plastic container and freeze for about 2 hours. Remove the sorbet, beat thoroughly to remove ice granules and return the sorbet to the freezing compartment. Twenty minutes before serving, remove the sorbet and divide into dishes or glasses and allow to rest in the refrigerator.

Cheesecake

Serves 6 (113 calories per person)

Pour the Grapenuts into a 7in (18cm) flan dish and spread evenly over the bottom. Mix the low-fat cheese with the yogurt and add the lemon rind, leaving aside 1tsp/5ml of grated rind for decoration. Add the low-calorie sweetener. Sprinkle the gelatine into the lemon juice and leave to set for 5 minutes. Then stand in a saucepan of simmering water and stir until it becomes a clear liquid. Do not allow to boil. Let the lemon and gelatine cool a little and then whisk it and the yolk into the cheese. Beat the whites until they peak and then fold them into the cheese mixture. Spoon carefully on to the Grapenut base and allow to set in the refrigerator for 2–3 hours. Decorate with the remainder of the grated lemon rind.

2oz/56g Grapenuts
1 × 6oz/175g packet low-fat soft cheese
1 × 5.3oz/150g carton natural yogurt
low-calorie sweetener equivalent to 2tbsp/30ml sugar
juice and finely grated rind of 2 lemons
1 egg yolk
2 egg whites
½oz/14g gelatine

Cold Lemon Soufflé

Serves 4 (113 calories per person)

Separate eggs and whisk egg yolks with the sweetener until they are light and fluffy. Beat the cheese, add the lemon rind and whisk in the egg yolks. Mix the lemon juice and gelatine together and beat over a pan of hot water until the gelatine dissolves. Cool and add to the lemon mixture. Beat egg whites until they peak and add to lemon. Put into a small soufflé dish around which you have stuck a circle of paper which is about 2in (5cm) higher than the rim. Put in the refrigerator for at least an hour until thoroughly set. Gently remove paper band so that the soufflé stands up above the dish and serve.

2 eggs
1 egg white
1oz/28g granulated low-calorie sweetener
4oz/113g low-fat soft cheese
grated rind and juice of 2 lemons
½oz/14g gelatine

Dried Fruit in Yogurt and Ginger

Serves 1 (150 calories per person)

Chop the fruit finely and mix with the ginger and the yogurt. Allow to rest in the refrigerator for at least 2 hours before serving. This makes a surprisingly rich and tasty sweet which can be adapted to choice with dates or sultanas, but see calorie guide in Appendix 1.

1 × 5.3oz/150g carton natural yogurt
2 dried pears
3 dried apricots
½tsp/2.5ml fresh grated ginger

Fresh Fruit Salad

Serves 4 (60 calories per person)

1 orange
1 apple
1 small banana
10 grapes
1 kiwi fruit
low-calorie lemonade

Peel and chop the orange and banana, slice the apple and de-pip the grapes. Mix together with a little low-calorie lemonade and decorate with the peeled, sliced kiwi fruit. This is a basic all-seasons recipe which can be adapted according to whatever fruit is available, using the calorie count in Appendix 1 as a guide.

Gooseberry Fool

Serves 4 (66 calories per person)

1lb/450g gooseberries
2oz/56g low-fat soft cheese
2 egg whites
low-calorie sweetener
grated nutmeg (optional)

Top and tail the gooseberries and cook in a little water until soft. Drain and put through a wide-mesh strainer. Beat the soft cheese, add the gooseberries and sweeten to taste. Whip the egg whites until peaks form and fold into the fool. Allow to cool and serve with a little grated nutmeg, if liked. Other fruits such as rhubarb can be treated in the same way.

Granite: Italian Water Ices

• It was the Chinese not the Italians who invented the water ice since it was they who first discovered the method of freezing blocks of ice underground. Nonetheless, today it is the Italians who have perfected the art of making *granite* or water ices. These are extremely simple to make but demand fresh fruit. They are simply a mixture of crushed ice and fruit purée. In addition, of course, there is the coffee water ice – *Granita al Caffé*.

Lemon Granita

Serves 4 (125 calories per person)

juice of 3 lemons
½pt/300ml water
1oz/28g granulated low-calorie sweetener

Mix the low-calorie sweetener and water in a pan and heat for a few minutes until dissolved. Cool and add the lemon juice. Taste for sweetness. I personally like my water ices slightly sharp but if you prefer a sweeter taste, then add some liquid sweetener at this point. Pour into an ice-cream tray or plastic freezer box, cover and freeze. About every 30 minutes give the ice a good stir and after 2–3 hours, the water ice should be a perfect mush. Spoon into glasses (the Italians use tall, narrow glasses) and serve with both a spoon and a straw.

Fruit Granita

Serves 4 (145–150 calories per person)

Pears Poached in Red Wine – a low-calorie sweet that is ideal for dinner parties; serve with natural yogurt or fromage frais but not cream (page 108)

Follow the above method but make a purée of 1lb/450g soft fruit such as strawberries (145 calories per person), raspberries (145 calories per person), blackberries (150 calories per person), or blackcurrants (150 calories per person) which should be strained and mixed with the juice of 1 lemon.

Granita al Caffé

Serves 4 (56 calories per person)

Make 1pt/600ml coffee, double the usual strength and sweeten with low-calorie sweetener. Freeze and serve as Lemon Granita (page 106). The Italians sometimes make this by pouring the sweetened strong coffee over crush ice. An instant refresher!

The Fruit Granite are particularly good served with a dribble of liqueur such as Kirsch and the Granita al Caffé blends excellently with brandy. (Allow 25–40 calories per dessertspoonful of liqueur – see Appendix 1.)

Mango Fool

Serves 3 (51 calories per person)

1 mango
1oz/28g low-fat soft cheese
1 egg white
Grated orange rind (optional)

Peel the mango, remove flesh and put through a fine strainer. Beat the soft cheese and add the mango. Whip the egg white until peaks form and fold into the fool. Serve sprinkled, if liked, with grated orange rind.

Pears Poached in Red Wine

Serves 4 (60 calories per person)
colour photograph page 107

4 pears
6fl oz/170ml dry red wine
½tsp/2.5ml ground cinnamon
low-calorie sweetener equivalent to 2tsp/10ml sugar

Peel the pears and place in a saucepan with the other ingredients. Bring to the boil for a couple of minutes to allow the alcohol to evaporate. Then poach gently for another 5 minutes, turning the pears so that they are evenly covered by the wine. Serve with a little natural yogurt sprinkled with cinnamon if wished.

Pêches Cardinal

Serves 2 (50 calories per person)

2 fresh peaches
4oz/113g fresh raspberries
low-calorie sweetener

• This dish can be altered depending on what fruits are in season. You can serve poached pears with raspberry or blackberry purée or nectarines with strawberry purée – the variations are endless, and the calories very low. This is an infinitely better way of serving fruit than with whipped cream and the flavours of the fruit are much better without it.

Poach the peaches for 2–3 minutes in a little water. Remove the skin, allow to cool and cut in half. Remove the peach stones and place the peach halves in a glass serving dish. Pour over a purée made of the raspberries pushed through a strainer and sweetened to taste with a little low-calorie sweetener.

Hot Pineapple Soufflé

Serves 4 (170 calories per person)

Crush or preferably blend the pineapple until it forms a soft purée. Put aside. Melt the butter gently and make a roux with the flour. Add the water gradually, making a smooth white sauce. Add the pineapple and sweetener. Take off the heat. Separate the eggs and add the yolks to the pineapple. Add the extra egg white and beat the whites until they are stiff. Fold into the pineapple, pour into a soufflé dish. Put into a pre-heated oven (350°F, 180°C, Gas Mark 4) for 30–40 minutes until risen and fluffy. Serve at once.

- 6oz/170g pineapple, drained of all juice
- 1oz/28g butter
- 1oz/28g flour
- 3 eggs
- 4fl oz/113ml water
- 1 egg white
- sweetener equivalent to 1tbsp/15ml sugar

Pineapple with Port

(30 calories per slice)

Cut fresh pineapple into slices and sprinkle with port. This sweet is so delicious, it is hard to believe it is not fattening.

- 1 pineapple
- 4tbsp/60ml port

Pineapple Surprise

Serves 4 (168 calories per person)

Cut off the top of the pineapple just below the crown and cut enough off the bottom so that the fruit will stand up straight. Wash the outside. Using a sharp knife, cut out the fruit of the pineapple in chunks and mix with the other fruit which should be peeled and sliced. In the case of the grapes remove the pips but not the skin. Pour over the sweet white wine. Allow to stand and before serving pile the fruit back into the pineapple, replace the crown and place in a dish with the remainder of the fruit salad around it.

- 1 small pineapple
- 1 orange
- 2 peaches
- 4oz/113g grapes
- 4fl oz/113ml sweet white wine (1 wineglass)

Rhubarb Meringue

Serves 4 (24 calories per person)

Wash rhubarb and remove any strings. Cut into short pieces and stew in a small amount of water until they are soft. Put into an ovenproof dish and allow to cool. Add liquid sweetener to taste. Whip the egg whites until peaks form. Mix with enough sweetener to equal 1tbsp/15ml of sugar and pour this meringue over the rhubarb. Cook in a cool oven (275°F, 150°C, Gas Mark 1) for 2 hours until the meringue is firm.

- 2lb/900g rhubarb
- 3 egg whites
- low-calorie sweetener

Rhubarb and Orange Compôte

Serves 4 (40 calories per serving)

Mix sweetener with 2tbsp/30ml water and stir until dissolved. Wash the rhubarb and cut into small chunks; place in a casserole with the oranges, peeled and sliced. Add the sweetened water and cook in a medium oven (350°F, 180°C, Gas Mark 4) for 20 to 25 minutes until it is cooked but not squashy.

- 1lb/450g rhubarb
- 2 oranges
- low-calorie sweetener equivalent to 4tbsp/60ml sugar

Saffron Rice with Raisins

Serves 4 (109 calories per person)

2oz/56g long grain rice
1tbsp/15ml lemon juice
low-calorie sweetener
¼tsp/1.25ml cinnamon
½tsp/2.5ml saffron
8 almonds
4fl oz/113ml orange juice
2oz/56g raisins
1tbsp/15ml orange flower water
Grated orange rind to decorate

• This is an unusual sweet and much lighter than the English rice pudding. It incorporates the Persian love for dried fruits and the way in which their cuisine mixes flavours.

First take the saffron, which should be in strands, not powdered (the latter is frequently not pure saffron) and allow to soak in water to bring out the full colour and flavour. Then cook the rice as you would for savoury rice, using whatever is your favourite method and using the saffron and its water. When the rice is tender allow to stand. Mix together the sweetener, the cinnamon, the lemon juice and the orange juice and heat for a few moments until the sweetener has completely dissolved. Pour over the rice and add the raisins, stirring well until all the rice is thoroughly mixed. Allow to cool and serve with the orange flower water and the almonds, finely chopped, sprinkled on top. A little grated orange rind also makes a colourful and tasty decoration.

Strawberries in Yogurt

Serves 4 (63 calories per person)

1lb/450g strawberries
liquid sweetener (optional)
1 × 10.6oz/300g carton natural yogurt
mint leaves

Wash and hull the strawberries and allow to drain thoroughly. Mix with the yogurt and add liquid sweetener if you need it. I, personally, prefer the natural taste of strawberries. Place in serving glasses and decorate with fresh mint leaves.

Tipsy Melon

Serves 4 (80 calories per person)

1 small canteloupe melon
2tbsp/30ml Cointreau or other liqueur
lemon balm to decorate (optional)

Cut the top off the melon, scoop out the seeds and remove the flesh in balls. Pour the liqueur over the melon balls and allow to marinate. Before serving replace in melon shell and decorate if wished with lemon balm. You can also make this dish attractive by cutting the melon into a basket to serve. Ideal for a dinner party.

Zabaglione

Serves 4 (100 calories per person)

4 egg yolks
granulated low-calorie sweetener equivalent to 4tsp/20ml sugar
6fl oz/170ml Marsala

Beat the egg yolks and the low-calorie sweetener together in a bowl held over a pan of hot water or a double-boiler until they are frothy. Add the Marsala slowly until they form a creamy-smooth custard. Do not allow it to boil or it will curdle. As soon as it turns into a custard pour into glasses and serve immediately.

·Stocks·Sauces·and·Dressings·

STOCKS

Basic Stock

If you are cooking with less fat then the quality of your stock is even more important. When you are in a hurry you cannot start making stock before cooking a meal and therefore it makes a lot of sense to have some stock prepared. Stock freezes well and is particularly useful if you reduce it so that it is quite rich and you can then freeze it in ice cube trays.

Roughly chop the vegetables and put in a deep pan with the other ingredients. Add plenty of water and bring to the boil and simmer for 4 to 5 hours on a low heat making sure that there is enough water. Strain and allow to cool. Remove any fat from the top and return to a pan. Boil briskly for 30 minutes until the stock has reduced to half its quantity. Use or freeze.

For a good basic stock take:

3lb/1350g beef bones for a beef stock or chicken bones and carcass for a chicken stock or fish heads and bones for a fish stock. For a vegetable stock just use the ingredients below and any other tired vegetables you have hanging around your kitchen.
2 carrots
1 onion
2 sticks celery
1 clove garlic
2 leeks
2tbsp/30ml chopped parsley
2tsp/10ml chopped dried thyme

Seafood Stock

Peel the prawns and put these aside to use elsewhere. Take the prawn shells and cover with water. Add the white wine. Bring to the boil and simmer for 30 minutes, bashing the shells now and again to break them up. When the shells are greyish and most of the colour is in the liquid, strain and return the liquid to the pan. Boil for another 10 minutes until the liquid has reduced by half. Use or freeze.

8oz/226g peeled prawns
4fl oz/113ml dry white wine
(1 wineglass)

SAUCES

Basic White Sauce

1oz/28g cornflour
½pt/300ml skimmed milk

This is simply thickened milk and is much too bland to use on its own, though with the variations given below it makes a perfectly adequate and very light sauce. It uses far less calories than the basic roux method, though the roux can also be made less fattening by using a low-calorie spread instead of butter and water instead of milk. I use water in white sauces and soufflés because I find it makes them lighter.

Take a couple of spoonfuls of the milk and mix it with the cornflour to form a smooth paste. Heat the rest of the milk until it is almost boiling and gradually pour this onto the paste, stirring well, until you have a smooth sauce. Then season and add any of the following:

Cheese Sauce

(563 calories) Serves 4–6 (93–140 calories per person)

Add 2oz/56g grated Cheddar, 1oz/28g grated Parmesan and ½tsp/2.5ml made-up mild mustard.

Dutch Cheese Sauce

(500 calories) Serves 4–6 (83–125 calories per person)

2oz/56g grated Edam and ½tsp/2.5ml freshly grated nutmeg.

Parsley Sauce

(210 calories) Serves 4–6 (35–52 calories per person)

3tbsp/45ml finely chopped parsley.

Tarragon Sauce

(210 calories) Serves 4–6 (35–52 calories per person)

3tbsp/45ml finely chopped fresh tarragon or 1tbsp/15ml dried tarragon.

Egg Sauce

Serves 4–6 (43–72 calories per person)

1 hardboiled egg, finely chopped and 2tbsp/30ml chopped chives.

Mushroom Sauce

(228 calories) Serves 4 (57 calories per person)

1oz/28g low-calorie spread
1oz/28g plain flour
2oz/56g mushrooms
juice of 1 lemon
salt and pepper

ROUX METHOD
Finely chop the mushrooms. Mix together the low-calorie spread and lemon juice in a small saucepan and heat the mushrooms gently for 2–3 minutes. Remove from the heat and sieve in the flour little by little, stirring well until it forms a roux. Return to the heat and gradually add water, stirring constantly until you have a smooth sauce. Season well.
Note This sauce is even better with a little fresh tarragon and garlic which should be added to the mushrooms.

Onion Sauce

(355 calories) Serves 4–6 (59–88 calories per person)

Finely chop the onion and sweat in the oil for 5 minutes until soft. Sprinkle on the flour and stir well until you have a roux. Gradually add the milk, stirring constantly, and simmer for another 5 minutes until the sauce is thick and smooth. Season well with plenty of salt and freshly ground black pepper.

1 medium onion
1oz/28g plain flour
½pt/300ml skimmed milk
1tbsp/15ml cooking oil
salt and freshly ground black pepper

Caraway Sauce

(130 calories) Serves 4–6 (21–32 calories per person)

Melt the low-fat spread and add the flour, stirring well. Add the caraway seeds. Return to the heat and gradually add the stock, stirring constantly until you have a smooth sauce.

1oz/28g low-fat spread
1oz/28g plain flour
½pt/300ml meat stock
1tsp/5ml caraway seeds

Italian Tomato Sauce

(235 calories) Serves 4 (58 calories per person)

Finely chop the onion and green pepper and sweat in the oil for 5 minutes. Add the can of tomatoes together with the tomato purée, the herbs and salt and pepper and simmer for 10 minutes or so until the sauce has reduced and has a good thick consistency.

1 medium onion
1 green pepper
1tbsp/15ml cooking oil
1 × 14oz/396g can tomatoes
1tbsp/15ml tomato purée
1tsp/5ml dried basil
1tsp/5ml dried oregano
salt and pepper

Chinese-style Barbecue Sauce

(286 calories) Serves 4 (71 calories per person)

Pour the tomato ketchup and the soy sauce into a bowl and gradually stir in the honey, the red wine vinegar and orange juice. Season with the Tabasco, crushed garlic, celery salt and plenty of freshly ground black pepper. This sauce is particularly good for marinating chicken pieces or spare ribs prior to grilling them. It also makes a good sauce for sausages and other barbecued grills.

2tbsp/30ml clear honey
2tbsp/30ml soy sauce
4tbsp/60ml low-calorie tomato ketchup
few drops Tabasco sauce
2 cloves garlic
½tsp/2.5ml celery salt
4tbsp/60ml red wine vinegar
juice of 1 orange
freshly ground black pepper

Tomato Sauce

Serves 1 (74 calories per person)

Pour the can of tomatoes into a small saucepan and add the herbs, the garlic, crushed, and the onion and the pepper, finely chopped. Simmer for 5 minutes and add the tomato purée. Simmer for another 10 minutes adding a little water if it looks too dry. Serve with any form of pasta, with meatloaf, with jacket potatoes or rice.

1 × 10oz/284g can tomatoes
1 small onion
½ chopped green pepper
1 clove garlic
1tsp/5ml Italian dried herbs
2tbsp/30ml tomato purée

Sweet Sauces

Fruit sauces are delicious and there is nothing nicer than the delicate combination of two different kinds of fruit such as you will find in the French Pêches Cardinal (p108) recipe. The basis of all these sauces is fresh fruit, so take whatever is in season. Strain and sweeten with low-calorie sweetener to taste and make up your own combinations such as pears with blackberries, stewed apples with peaches and peaches with blackcurrants.

DRESSINGS

Yogurt Dressing

(100 calories) Serves 2–3 (33–50 calories per person)

1 × 5.3oz/150g carton natural yogurt
2tbsp/30ml lemon juice
½tsp/2.5ml cumin seeds
salt and freshly ground black pepper

• This is my everyday salad dressing, particularly good with white cabbage.

Gradually add the lemon juice to the yogurt and stir in the cumin. Season with salt and plenty of freshly ground black pepper.
Variation: For Herby Yogurt Dressing, replace the cumin seeds with chopped chives, parsley, thyme, mint or marjoram.

Orange and Mustard Dressing

(40 calories) Serves 2 (20 calories per person)

juice of 1 orange *or*
3.5fl oz/100ml orange juice
2tsp/10ml made coarse-grained mild mustard
½tsp/2.5ml cumin seeds or caraway seeds (optional)

Mix the orange juice with the mustard and add the spices if wanted. This will depend on the salad, eg caraway seeds are great with carrots and celery and cumin marvellous with cabbage. But experiment and find out what you enjoy. This is a versatile and very low-calorie dressing.

French Dressing

Serves 2 (128 calories per person)

2tbsp/30ml olive oil
3tbsp/45ml wine vinegar
1tsp/5ml made-up mild mustard
low-calorie sweetener equivalent to 1tsp/5ml sugar
1 clove garlic
salt and freshly ground black pepper

Crush the garlic and mix with the mustard. Add the sweetener and stir well. Gradually add the oil and vinegar and mix well together. Season with salt and plenty of freshly ground black pepper. The easiest way to mix well is to put all the ingredients into a small screw-top jar and shake well.
Variation: For Herby French Dressing, add 1tbsp/15ml fresh chopped herbs such as thyme.

Cider Vinegar Dressing

Serves 4 (18 calories per person)

¼pt/150ml apple juice
2tbsp/30ml cider vinegar
½tsp/2.5ml made-up mild mustard
1tbsp/15ml fresh chopped herbs
salt and freshly ground black pepper

Mix the cider vinegar with the mustard and gradually add the apple juice. Stir in the herbs and season with salt and freshly ground black pepper.

Tomato Dressing

Serves 4 (26 calories per person)

Whip the yogurt and gradually add the tomato juice and lemon juice. Stir in the parsley and season to taste with salt and freshly ground black pepper.

1 × 5.3oz/150g carton natural yogurt
4fl oz/113ml tomato juice
1tbsp/15ml lemon juice
1tbsp/15ml fresh chopped parsley
salt and freshly ground black pepper

Slimmer's Mayonnaise

(210 calories) Serves 2 (105 calories per person)

• This is a thicker sauce ideal with cold fish or vegetables.

Pound the egg yolks and beat in the mustard. Gradually add the lemon juice and oil until you have a smooth sauce. Season with salt and pepper.

2 egg yolks (hardboiled)
1tsp/5ml mild mustard
juice of 1 lemon
2tsp/10ml olive oil
salt and pepper

Yogurt Mayonnaise

(265 calories) Serves 4–6 (44–66 calories per person)

• This is a good general alternative to mayonnaise for all kinds of salads.

Mash the egg yolk and mix with the lemon juice until it forms a smooth paste, then gradually add the yogurt. Season with salt and pepper.

1 egg yolk (hardboiled)
2 × 5.3fl oz/150g cartons natural yogurt
2tbsp/30ml lemon juice
salt and pepper

Curry Mayonnaise

Serves 4 (2tbsp/30ml and 60 calories per person)

• This goes particularly well with cold chicken.

Mix the mayonnaise with the yogurt. Press the ginger through a garlic press and mix with the mayonnaise and the curry powder. Season with pepper.

4tbsp/60ml low-calorie mayonnaise
1 × 5.3oz/150g carton natural yogurt
1 sliver fresh ginger
½tsp/2.5ml mild curry powder
pepper

Chive Dressing

(140 calories) Serves 4 (35 calories per person)

Pound the egg yolk and mix with oil until it forms a smooth paste. Finely chop the white and mix this and the chives with the yolk. Gradually add the lemon juice and water and season to taste. This is a good dressing for many vegetables, especially cooked vegetables and cold chicken and fish.

1 hardboiled egg
½tsp/2.5ml olive oil
1tbsp/15ml chopped chives
juice of ½ lemon
2tbsp/30ml water
salt and pepper

·Drinks·

colour photograph page 119

However carefully you measure what you eat, it is all too easy to imbibe a few hundred calories unknowingly with the most innocent-looking drinks. Orange juice, for example, is not as innocent as it seems when a mere 4fl oz/43ml – just a wineglass – can go from 30 calories (for the calorie reduced) to 60 calories (reconstituted frozen) and 80 for a sweetened variety. The drinks given below will help you avoid this liquid liability.

NON-ALCOHOLIC

HERB TEAS OR TISANES

Herb teas are not only low calorie but are also remedies for common complaints from sore throats to indigestion. Almost every herb and spice has been used by peasants and apothecaries in an infusion in some country and the following are simply a selection. Many people will tell you that these herbs need to be infused or simmered but I find that they are perfectly adequate made like ordinary tea. Just throw the herbs into a warmed teapot, pour on the boiling water and allow to stew for about 5 minutes. Strain and sweeten if necessary with honey, allowing about 20 calories per level teaspoon/5ml.

Camomile Tea

The aroma of camomile is one of the essential smells of the Mediterranean, but I was first given camomile tea in the North of France where its all-heal qualities are still respected. In Italy and Greece it is also well loved and again it is the Greek stores and also Culpeppers, that sell the best dried camomile flowers. A handful of these thrown in the pot, made in the usual way, is the most soothing of night-time drinks. In addition camomile is good for sore throats, indigestion, colds and almost everything else. An old Cretan lady I know used to make a strong brew which she would allow to cool. Then she would dip in pads of cotton wool and lay these on my eyes. I have never found a quicker or better pick-me-up and thoroughly recommend it to anyone suffering from eye strain or exhaustion.

Dandelion Tea

Ancient Arab writers as well as English herbalists have recommended the dandelion and its leaves are widely appreciated in salads in most countries apart from Great Britain. The tea is said to have diuretic properties and held to be good for dieters. The tea ideally should be made with dried leaves. Pick a good bunch of young dandelion leaves, wash and dry them and allow them to hang in a warm kitchen until dry. Then crumble them as you would any other dried herb. This tea does need sweetening. Use a low-calorie sweetener.

Mint Tea

I cannot think about Morocco without remembering the smell and taste of the sweet mint tea which is given to you in every shop and house. Peppermint is particularly good for indigestion and the best tea is made with the dried flowers – not the kind of mint you use for your mint sauce. Dried peppermint is available in most Greek stores and many health food shops. It is also available in tea bags but this does not taste as good. The Moroccans drink their mint tea very sweet but I find that 1tsp/5ml of honey is perfectly adequate to sweeten one cup.

Rosemary Tea

This herb tea is helpful to sore throats and I find it very soothing when I have a cold.

Sage Tea

It is the Germans who favour sage and it is an excellent general health tea said to be particularly good for stress and shock. Make in the usual way and sweeten with honey if desired.

Other Herb Teas
Many other herbs make good tisanes. Marjoram is said to help induce sleep and, like thyme, is excellent for nervous headaches. Thyme tea is also said to help coughs, colds and colic and in the Mediterranean it has long been thought to be a cure for depression. All these teas are cheap and soothing and the best thing is to taste, try and mix your own until you find the blend you prefer. As a night-time drink they are infinitely better than hot chocolate! Herb tea is also delicious cold and poured over ice cubes. Serve with a few fresh leaves of mint and borage flowers if you have any.

My own magic mixture of herb tea is as follows: Make up a dried mixture using in proportion 2tbsp/30ml of peppermint flowers with 2tsp/10ml dried sage and 2tsp/10ml dried rosemary. Mix well together and allow 1tbsp/15ml per pot. I do not find that I need any sweetening with this mixture although you can add honey if you want. This tea is particularly good served cold and poured over ice cubes on a hot day.

COOL DRINKS

Grapefruit Cooler
This is one of my favourite drinks and very refreshing on hot days. Serve one part grapefruit juice to two parts soda or perrier water, adding a couple of fresh mint leaves to each glass. Allow about 50 calories for each 4fl oz/113ml of unsweetened grapefruit juice.

Sparkling St Clements
For a zingy citrus drink, mix the juice of one lemon with a bottle of low-calorie fizzy orange. Pour over ice cubes and serve with a strip of orange peel. For 2 people it will cost a mere 7 calories each.

Virgin Mary
This is a good pub drink and also, I find, an excellent hangover cure. It is simply a Bloody Mary without the vodka: simply add Worcester sauce, tabasco and a twist of lemon to your glass of tomato juice. At 30 calories for 4fl oz/113ml, it is less than half the alcoholic version.

LOW CALORIE SHAKES

Quantities for these shakes are given for one person with the calories accordingly. The basis of these low-calorie shakes is ¼pt/150ml of skimmed milk, 2 or 3 ice cubes and low-calorie sweetener to taste. Put all the ingredients together in a liquidiser and blend until they become frothy.

Coffee Shake *(60 calories)*
Put all the ingredients as above plus 1tsp/5ml of instant coffee into the liquidiser and serve with the merest dusting of drinking chocolate.

Strawberry Shake *(70 calories)*
Add 5 fresh strawberries or 1tbsp/15ml unsweetened or low-calorie canned strawberries.

Peach Shake *(85 calories)*
Add 1 peeled and stoned fresh peach.

Chocolate Shake *(80 calories)*
Mix 1tsp/5ml drinking chocolate with a little of the milk until it forms a paste and slowly add the milk to this before liquidising. Serve with a small sprinkling of freshly ground nutmeg.

Luxury Milk Shake
Add 1oz/28g vanilla ice cream to any of the above milk shakes and another 50 calories to the total.

WINES AND SPIRITS

This is the danger for so many people who are trying to cut calories. It is a good idea to remember that the stronger the drink, the more calories it will have. Mixing a little alcohol with a non-alcoholic and non-calorific drink is therefore a clever way to cut down calories. As long as the drink tastes alcoholic, you won't notice the fact that it is blended with a mixer. Long drinks are preferable and more satisfying. My own favourite in the following list is the dry Martini and a dry Martini with slimline tonic at a pub is an ideal low-calorie drink. One word of warning, however; if you order a dry Martini in the USA, you will get the vermouth ready mixed with gin which is considerably more calories.

Spritzer
Dry white wine is the slimmer's favourite but is not as innocent as it appears. Indeed, a measure or 4fl oz/113ml only half fills a large wineglass and a full glass, double this quantity, will set you back 150 calories. And it's not difficult to drink two glasses, especially on a hot day. The Americans have come up with the answer in the Spritzer, which is a combination of chilled white wine and soda water. I make the mixture half and half and serve it very cold. This way you can have a full sparkling glass for 75 calories and bubble virtuously.

Kir
A low-calorie Kir is a version of a Spritzer. Simply add a few drops of crème de cassis to your dry white wine and top up with soda water. Using a tsp/5ml of crème de cassis and 4fl oz/113ml dry white wine, this Kir will only cost you 85 calories, less than a pub measure of sweet Martini.

Dry Martini
This is by no means the James Bond version and it should most certainly be stirred not shaken. Forget anything you ever heard about pouring on the gin and holding the dry Martini. In this version you add the dry Martini and hold the gin. Fill a tumbler with ice cubes, pour in a capful of dry Martini, top up with low-calorie tonic and serve with a good twist of lemon. A good long drink for a mere 60 calories. An alternative slightly sweeter drink can be made using Cinzano Bianco and in this case serve with a twist of orange and allow yourself 80 calories.

Sherry on the Rocks
Dry sherry, and I mean a dry fino, not the medium-dry kind, is only 55 calories for a schooner. Pour this over a tumblerful of cracked ice and you will have a low calorie and cooling drink.

COCKTAILS

Cocktails are notorious diet breakers, not only in themselves, but because the two-Martini lunch will doubtless include all the things you've been banning yourself for the last few weeks. Nevertheless, for the strong minded the occasional cocktail is a pleasure most of us enjoy. I include here a few of the less-fattening cocktails which hail from the Caribbean.

Rum Punch
It is essential to have fresh limes, although Culpeppers do bottle an excellent pure lime juice. Simply mix a measure of white rum with a measure of fresh lime juice and pour over cracked ice. Garnish with a twist of lime and a sprig of mint and add as little or as much soda water as you wish. This will only cost you 60 calories.

Cuba Libre
For a mere 50 calories add a single measure of white rum to low-calorie cola such as Diet Coke or Diet Pepsi. Serve with a good wedge of fresh lime and plenty of ice.

Peach Daquiri
This is one of my all-time favourite summer drinks. Liquidise a whole peach with low-calorie sweetener equivalent to 1tsp/5ml sugar and shake this with a single measure of white rum. Pour over ice in a large tumbler and fill up with soda. It will cost you 100 calories but tastes like 1,000! Incidentally, you can do the same thing with strawberries for even less calories!

From Russia with Love
Vodka is an excellent mixer, although personally I prefer the flavoured Russian kind which, unfortunately, is twice as high in calories. However, this is drunk in very small glasses as it is swigged not sipped and a single measure of lemon vodka is 100 calories. Vodka should be served ice cold and a Russian hint to improve your ordinary vodka is to pour it into a heavy glass decanter, add a few very thin slivers of lemon or orange peel and put it into your freezing compartment for about 10 minutes before serving. Don't let it freeze. The two following Russian cocktails were given to me by an emigré Russian in Paris many years ago.

Vishnyovky Cocktail
In Russia, as throughout the Balkans and in Greece, every summer the old ladies get to work stoning the cherries (a deft use is made of hairpins here) and covering them with sugar and alcohol. This drink is made with the same ingredients but without allowing the cherries to ferment. Stalk and stone 2oz/56g of ripe cherries and liquidise with 1tsp/5ml of sugar. Mix with a single measure of plain vodka and serve very cold with plenty of ice: 100 calories.

Balalaika Cocktail
Mix together 2fl oz/56ml orange juice with a single measure of vodka. Chill well and serve in a tumbler topped up with soda water: 70 calories.

You can easily drink a day's calorific needs without noticing it, but home-made low-calorie drinks are delicious; when it comes to alcohol, moderation is the watchword

·Herbs·and·Spices·

Allspice
West Indian spice so called because it is said to combine the flavour of cinnamon, nutmeg and cloves. It is also known as Jamaica Pepper and is widely used throughout the Caribbean. Best known over here as a pickling spice, its flavour is strong, so use sparingly.

Anise
Anyone familiar with aniseed balls will need no introduction to this herb. It is one of the best of all herbs to aid digestion, especially when made as aniseed tea and the star anise has the same liquorice flavour. It's too strong to use widely in cooking although it can be added to curries.

Balm
Balm is useful for decorating summer drinks and sorbets. Finely chopped, the leaves can also be used in salad dressings and if you happen to be cooking sponge cakes – for the rest of the family no doubt – you can infuse them with a delightful lemony flavour by laying a couple of balm leaves on the bottom of the cake tin while cooking.

Basil
A pot of basil is found in almost every Mediterranean garden and on every city balcony. It is most widely used in Italy because of its perfect marriage with tomatoes. It also goes well with cooked cheese and its fresh leaves will enliven any salad.

Bay
A leaf or two is common in soups, stews, sauces and to make a bouquet garni. A bay leaf in a flour bin keeps out weevils.

Borage
Both the leaves and flowers of borage with their cucumber flavour can be used in the kitchen. Borage flowers are wonderful in summer drinks; try them with cider and the leaves finely chopped are good in soups, salad and sauces.

Caraway
Although it is best known on bread and cakes, I prefer caraway with savoury dishes – many found in Eastern Europe – such as with cabbage, carrots and in soups.

Cardamon
This spice is widely used in the Middle East, Pakistan and India. It is best known as an ingredient of curries although its distinctive, pungent flavour is better when not masked by other spices. In the Middle East it is added to coffee and used in cakes. Chew on a seed to remove the taste of garlic and onions.

Celery
We know it as a vegetable but in many parts of Europe its leaves, fresh or dried, are used as a herb. Excellent in soups and also ideal for stuffing a chicken. Take a handful of dried celery leaves with a few sprigs of thyme and insert in the chicken before roasting. The flavour will permeate the whole bird.

Chervil
Along with chives, parsley and tarragon, chervil makes up the famous *fines herbes*, although its aniseed-flavoured leaves are less widely used. Use it in salads, soups, and to enliven scrambled eggs and always add the herb just before serving.

Chives
What would I do without my perennial clump of chives? With their delicate onion flavour, they are invaluable in salads, soufflés, soups and sauces. Finely chopped, they enliven cottage cheese, scrambled eggs, potatoes and can decorate almost every savoury dish you bring to the table.

Cinnamon
One of the most widely used of all spices, it is available in stick form or ready ground. Sprinkle it of course on apples, yogurts and other sweets, but also use it in savoury dishes – a small pinch brings out the flavour of mince whether in an Italian Bolognese sauce or Shepherd's Pie.

Cloves
Used in pickling, delicious when used in moderation with apples and in custards.

Coriander
As parsley is in the West, so coriander is in the East. It is used, both leaf and seed, in cooking from the Middle East to South East Asia and the leaves are widely used as a garnish. The seed can be used ground to add fragrance to all spicy dishes.

Cumin
This herb has a wonderful aromatic flavour in cabbage salads, rice salads, with many cooked vegetables, in soups, with pulses and when baked in bread, as they do on the island of Crete. Sausages are wonderful flavoured with cumin and so are meatballs. Buy the seeds and crush them yourself as the flavour is much better than the ready ground and, of course, the seeds will last, unlike the powder. If you come across recipes calling for sweet cumin, this is not cumin but fennel.

Dill
I wish we could buy bunches of fresh dill in greengrocers as you can in Europe; this feathery-leaved plant, more delicate than the fennel leaf, is delicious chopped in salads, especially tomato salad.

Fennel
Fennel is used fresh and dried and its aniseed flavour is good for vegetable and meat dishes as well as the better known accompaniment for fish.

Garlic
The number of recipes in this book which include garlic should indicate the pleasure I derive from this bulb. Cut it in slivers and insert it in your leg of lamb; use it in salads, sauces and stews. Or mash it with hardboiled egg yolks and add a little oil and some lemon juice to make Aioli, a wonderful sauce that will go with almost anything from fish to chicken, from roast beef to boiled potatoes. Make a slimmer's garlic bread by mixing low-calorie spread with crushed garlic, spreading along the sides of a French loaf cut almost through, which is then wrapped in foil and heated in a hot oven for about 10 minutes. To counteract its flavour on your breath, chew cardamon seeds.

Ginger
Forget the powdered stuff you buy in little bottles. It has little in common with the sweet and pungent flavour of the freshly cut ginger root. This is now widely available and should be sliced or grated. Fresh ginger can be found in some ethnic stores and this is naturally juicier with a fresher flavour.

Juniper
Best known for the making of gin, juniper berries arè excellent with pork and game and sublime with sauerkraut. Crush them slightly before use to bring out the flavour. I bake pork chops (having cut off as much of the fat as possible) with apple juice and juniper berries, and also add them to red cabbage.

Lovage
Traditional British herb, the use of which has almost died out today. It is easy to grow and its celery-tasting leaves can be used in just the same way as parsley.

Marjoram
Marjoram and oregano belong to the same family. Marjoram (*Oreganum marjorana*) is known as sweet or knotted marjoram and oregano (*Oreganum vulgare*) is known as common or wild marjoram in Britain, oregano in Italy and rigani in Greece. There is also pot marjoram (*Oreganum onites*) in South East Europe and its leaves are also known as oregano. Sweet marjoram can be used to flavour meat, poultry and game and in omelettes and sauces. Oregano gives a stronger flavour when dried. It is widely used in Mediterranean cooking and ubiquitous in Greece. Pizzas, moussaka and pastas depend on it, though it should be used in moderation.

Mint
The common mint or spearmint (*Mentha spicata*) has many other uses besides accompanying roast lamb. Not only do potatoes benefit from it, but so do other vegetables such as parsnips, carrots, peas and beans. It goes well with many fruits. It is refreshing in sorbets and decorates many summer drinks. A cousin, the apple mint (*Mentha rotundiflora*) has an additional apple flavour and can be used in just the same way. Mint tea is made with the dried mauve flowers of the spearmint.

Mustard
An increasing number of good made mustards which use the ground rather than the powdered seed are now available. When using mustard seed – in curries and other hot dishes – use sparingly as it is very hot.

Nutmeg
I rarely serve cauliflower or leeks without a light dusting of freshly ground nutmeg. More than any other spice this must be fresh; grate a little on apple and cheese dishes and add it to casseroles and risottos.

Oregano see Marjoram

Paprika
In Hungary there are seven kinds of paprika from the delicate Kuloneges paprika to the fierce Eros paprika; it depends what part of the pepper is used and the amount of seeds. In Hungary it is used where we would use black pepper.

Parsley
Try growing the European flat-leaved variety as well as the crinkly British kind. Parsley should be used in much larger quantities – as it is in North Africa and the Middle East – and not be regarded as a garnish.

Pepper
There are many kinds of peppers from the sweet paprika to the fierce cayenne and chilli. In Mexico there are sixty-one classified varieties of chilli. The green chillies are hotter than the red and in fact somewhat lethal if not used circumspectly. White pepper has few uses today and black peppercorns should *always* be freshly ground. Green peppercorns (these can be found ready dried at Culpeppers) are excellent for Steak Tartare and in spicy Indian dishes. I also use them to make my own herb cheese: on a plate prepare 1tbsp/15ml of finely chopped chives, 2tbsp/30ml of finely chopped fresh thyme. Mix together 4oz/113g of curd cheese and 2oz/56g of cream cheese and with a fork mix with the herbs until they are evenly distributed. Divide in half and make into two little balls. Grind or crush 2tbsp/30ml of green peppercorns and roll each little cheese into this until the outside is covered. Cover and keep in the refrigerator until needed. This makes two cheeses at 210 calories each. You can, of course, change the flavour by adding garlic, ground juniper berries (put them in your peppermill) and any other herb or spice you fancy. As with any other use of herbs, experiment is the name of the game.

Rosemary
Very strong herb, delicious with roast lamb and in stuffings for poultry. Because of its strength it does not mix well with other herbs, but it is good crumbled on pork or lamb chops.

Saffron
The joy of the ancient Phoenicians, it is the basis of boullabaisse, paella and risotto Milanese. Its subtle flavour adds to Eastern cooking, but it is expensive.

Sage
Again a herb with a strong personality and generally kept for stuffing poultry and cooking with roast pork. Sage, however, is the perfect accompaniment to liver and it helps counteract the richness of other foods, especially fish. Sprinkle it into your vegetable soups and cook it with peas.

Savory
Medieval England knew savory well and enjoyed its peppery flavour. There are two plants, summer savory and winter savory, and both can be used in cooking. It goes particularly well with beans and in Holland and Germany is known as the 'bean herb'. Sprinkle it on soups and also use it in seafood dishes and with all pulses.

Sesame
These delicious seeds are unfortunately full of oil and will cost you 160 calories an ounce (28g). Their uses, too, are invariably fattening, such as the sesame-coated prawns of China which are deep fried and the Eastern European sesame cakes. Sesame seed emulsion (Tahini) is the basic ingredient of halva and hummous. To cut down on your salt intake mix crushed sesame seeds with natural salt and use this as an alternative. It is very good with vegetables.

Tarragon
The delicate flavour of tarragon is one of the most expressive of all herbs. Chop it with mushrooms and in mushroom soup, add it to spinach soufflés and put a couple of sprigs of the fresh herb inside your chicken before roasting. Tarragon is also good with fish, with egg dishes and an essential member of the French *fines herbes*. Pour cider vinegar over a few sprigs of fresh tarragon that you've placed in a glass bottle. Cork or seal well to make tarragon vinegar.

Thyme
The scent of thyme evokes the Mediterranean and it is not surprising that it was thought to be a herb of the sun. Use it fresh if possible in soups and sauces, with all kinds of meat and poultry and in many pulse dishes. It is extremely easy to grow and provides good ground cover. There are several kinds: the best known being the common thyme (*Thymus vulgaris*) the dark green plant, and lemon thyme (*Thymus citriodorus*). The latter has a delicate lemony taste and can be used with apples and fish and as a subtle accompaniment to chicken.

Turmeric
This bright yellow spice, popular in the East and invaluable in curries, comes from a root and is usually bought in powdered form; use sparingly.

·Appendices·

1 THE INGLEWOOD CALORIE AND FIBRE COUNTER

Fruits per oz/28g unless stated	**Calories**	**Fibre(g)**
Apple (average 4oz/113g)	61	2.3
Banana (average 6oz/170g)	78	3.4
Blackberries	8	2.1
Blackcurrants	8	2.5
Cherries	13	0.4
Damsons	10	1.0
Gooseberries	5	2.9
Grapes	14	0.3
Grapefruit (½ average)	15	0.5
Mango (1 average 4oz/113g)	20	1.5
Melon (average 8oz/226g slice)	30	1.0
Watermelon (average 8oz/226g slice)	124	–
Nectarine (1 average 4oz/113g)	54	2.4
Orange (1 average 5oz/140g)	35	2.1
Passion Fruit (1 average 3oz/84g)	12	5.5
Peach (1 average 4oz/113g)	40	1.4
Pear (1 average 4oz/113g)	33	1.9
Pineapple fresh	13	1.2
canned in natural juice	22	0.9
Plum (2.5oz/70g average size)	26	1.5
Raspberries raw	7	2.1
Redcurrants	6	2.3
Rhubarb raw	2	1.7
Strawberries	7	0.10
Tangerine (average 3oz/84g)	20	0.42

The basis of healthy eating – fresh fruit and vegetables

Dried Fruit per oz/28g

Apricots	52	6.8
Currants	69	0.8
Dates stoned	70	2.4
Figs	61	5.2
Prunes	46	4.6
Raisins	71	1.9
Sultanas	71	2.0

Vegetables per oz/28g

Artichokes Jerusalem	5	
Asparagus boiled	5	0.4
Aubergine raw	4	0.7
Runner beans cooked	5	0.8
Bean sprouts	3	0.8
Broccoli cooked	5	1.7
Baked beans	18	2.0
Broad beans	14	1.2
Brussels sprouts	6	0.8
Butter beans boiled	27	7.2
Cabbage raw	6	1.0
red cooked	3	0.7
white cooked	5	0.8
Carrots boiled	6	0.8
Cauliflower boiled	3	0.5
Chick peas (dry weight)	91	4.2
Celeriac	4	1.4
Celery	2	0.5
Cucumber	3	0.1
Leeks cooked	7	1.1
Lentils (dry weight)	87	3.3
Lettuce	3	0.4
Marrow cooked	2	0.1
Mushrooms raw	4	0.7
fried	60	1.1
Onion raw	6	0.3
fried	97	1.2
spring raw	10	0.8
Parsnips cooked	14	0.7
Peas fresh cooked	15	1.4
Peas fresh frozen	15	2.2
Peppers green raw	4	0.2
Potatoes boiled	22	0.2
raw peeled	24	0.6
mashed	34	0.2
baked	30	0.6
roast	45	–
chips	73	–
crisps	152	0.1
Radishes	4	0.2
Red kidney beans (dry weight)	77	7.1
Red kidney beans cooked	28	3.0
Spinach boiled	9	1.8
Split peas boiled	33	1.4
Sweetcorn canned	21	1.6
on the cob	36	1.3
Swede cooked	5	0.8
Tomatoes raw	4	0.4
fried	20	0.8
Turnips boiled	3	0.6
Watercress	4	0.9

Bread per oz/28g

Brown	63	1.4
White	63	0.7
Wholemeal	61	2.4
Hovis	65	1.3

Cheese per oz/28g

Aerobic Gouda	60	–
Brie	85	–
Caerphilly	116	–
Camembert	85	–
Cheddar	115	–
Cheshire	95	–
Cottage cheese	27	–
Danish Blue	101	–
Double Gloucester	105	–
Edam	86	–
Gorgonzola	112	–
Lancashire	109	–
Mozzarella	80	–
Parmesan	114	–
Philadelphia soft cheese	90	–
Red Leicester	120	–
Roquefort	99	–
Stilton	132	–

Fats per oz/28g

Butter, margarine, Flora	211	–
Gold, Outline, low-fat spreads	104	–
Lard	254	–
Oils	256	–

Cream per ½pt/285ml

Single	593	–
Double	1,286	–
Whipping	1,065	–
Canned	620	–

Grains per oz/28g

Bran	58	12.5
Barley	102	2.1
Oatmeal	114	2.0
Rye	96	–

Eggs 1 whole

Raw	80	–
Boiled	80	–
Fried	120	–
Poached	80	–
Scrambled	125	–

Meats per oz/28g unless stated

Bacon, 1 rasher fried	94	–
Bacon, 1 rasher grilled	83	–
Bacon gammon joint raw	66	–
Beef mince raw	62	–
Beef rump steak grilled	64	–
sirloin raw	76	–
sirloin roast	80	–
stewing steak raw	49	–
topside raw	51	–
Chicken raw	34	–
boiled no skin	52	–

meat and skin roast	61	–
Duck raw meat	34	–
roast meat and skin	62	–
Ham boiled no fat	47	–
canned	34	–
Lamb cutlets raw	117	–
chop (5oz/140g) grilled	355	–
leg raw	67	–
leg roast	74	–
shoulder raw	88	–
shoulder roast	93	–
Liver calf raw	43	–
chicken raw	38	–
ox	46	–
Pheasant raw	60	–
Pigeon raw	64	–
Pork chops loin grilled	94	–
leg raw	76	–
leg roast	80	–
Rabbit raw	35	–
Turkey	40	–
Ham	34	–
Sausages beef raw	84	–
grilled	75	–
Sausages pork raw	103	–
grilled	89	–
Turkey raw	30	–
roast no skin	39	–
Veal fillet raw	31	–
roast	64	–

Fish per oz/28g		
Cod fillets fresh	22	–
Cod steaks frozen	19	–
Crabmeat boiled	36	–
Haddock smoked	28	–
Herring grilled	56	–
Kipper	58	–
Mackerel smoked	73	–
Mackerel raw	63	–
Prawns shelled	30	–
Salmon poached	50	–
Trout poached	25	–
White fish – halibut, plaice	26	–

Pasta per oz/28g		
White pasta (raw weight)	105	0.9
Wholewheat (raw weight)	98	2.8

Rice per oz/28g before cooking		
Brown	96	1.4
White	102	0.8

Cereals per oz/28g		
All-Bran	78	7.9
Branflakes	86	5.0
Muesli	105	2.1
Porridge (dry weight)	113	0.2
Puffed Wheat	104	5.0
Shredded Wheat (each)	93	3.5
Special K	110	1.5
Weetabix	97	3.6

Milk per pt/600ml		
Semi-skimmed	276	–
Skimmed	198	–
Whole milk	390	–

Yogurt per 5.3oz/150g carton		
Flavoured	50	–
Fruit	120–150	–
Natural	80	–

Nuts per oz/28g		
Almonds	161	4.0
Brazils	176	2.5
Chestnuts	48	1.9
Coconuts	100	3.8
Peanuts	162	2.3
Hazelnuts	108	2.3
Walnuts	150	1.4

Beer, Cider or Lager per ½pt/300ml		
Bitter	90	–
Brown ale	185	–
Cider	100	–
Home brewed beer	120	–
Lager	90	–
Light ale	75	–
Mild ale	75	–
Non alcoholic lager	45	–
Pale ale	90	–
Special brew lager	200	–

Fruit Juices per 4fl oz/113ml		
Apple	40	–
Grape	60	–
Grapefruit		
canned unsweetened	35	–
in a carton	25	–
Orange		
canned unsweetened	35	–
in a carton	40	–
frozen	60	–
Pineapple	65	–
Tomato	25	–

Fruit squashes undiluted per fl oz/28ml		
Ribena	85	–
Lemon barley water	30	–
Lemon squash	30	–
Orange squash	35	–

Liqueurs average, per bar measure	85	–

Port and Sherry per bar measure		
Sherry dry	55	–
medium	60	–
sweet	70	–
Port	75	–

Spirits per bar measure		
Brandy	50	–
Gin	50	–
Rum	50	–
Vodka	50	–

Whisky	50	–	Rosé	80	–
			White dry	75	–
Wine per 4fl oz/113ml (1 wineglass)			sparkling	90	–
Red dry	80	–	sweet	100	–
sweet	95	–			

2 METRIC EQUIVALENTS

Equivalent Liquid Measures

British	*Metric*	*American*
1 quart	11.4 decilitres	1 quart 8 fluid oz (2½ pints)
1pt	5.7 dl	1¼ pints
½pt	2.85 dl	10fl oz (1¼ cups)
1 gill (5fl oz)	1.4 dl	5fl oz
1tbsp (⅝fl oz)	1.5 cl	⅓fl oz
1dsp (⅓fl oz)	1 cl	1 tablespoon
1tsp (⅙fl oz)	0.05 cl (5ml)	⅙fl oz
Metric	*British*	*American*
1 litre	35fl oz (1¾ pints)	35fl oz (2 pints + 8 US tbs)
½ litre (5dl)	17½fl oz (⅞ pint + 4tbs)	17½fl oz (1 pint + 4tbs)
¼ litre (2.5dl)	8¼fl oz (½ pint – 2tbs)	8½fl oz (½ pint – 1tbs)
1 centilitre (10ml)	½fl oz (1 dessertspoon)	¼fl oz (1tbs)
American	*Metric*	*British*
1 quart (32fl oz)	9.5 dl	32fl oz (1½ pints + 3tbs)
1 pint (16fl oz)	4.7 dl	16fl oz (¼ pint + 2tbs)
1 cup (½ pint, 8fl oz)	2.4 dl	8 fl oz (½ pint – 3tbs)
1tbs (less than ½fl oz)	1.5 cl	less than ½fl oz

Solid Measures

	English Measure	*English Weight*	*Metric*	*American*
flour	1 heaped tablespoon	1oz	30g	2½ tablespoons
	4 heaped tablespoons	4oz	110g	1 scant cup
sugar: caster,	1 teaspoon	¼oz	7.5g	1 teaspoon
brown,	1 flat tablespoon	1oz	30g	1½ tablespoons
granulated	7 flat tablespoons	7oz	200g	1 cup
sugar: icing	1 heaped tablespoon	1oz	30g	3 tablespoons
	4 heaped tablespoons	4oz	110g	1 scant cup
rice (raw)	1 tablespoon	1oz	30g	2 tablespoons
	6 rounded tablespoons	8oz	225g	1¼ cups
butter or fat	1 flat tablespoon	1oz (plus)	30g	2 tablespoons
	8 flat tablespoons	8oz	225g	1 cup
dry grated cheese	1 flat tablespoon	1oz	30g	1½ tablespoons
	1 teacup	3½oz	100g	⅔ cup
		5oz	140g	1 cup
fresh bread crumbs	1 teacup	3oz	85g	⅔ cup

Metric and American equivalents are approximate only

·Index·of·Recipes·